GREG NORMAN'S
100
INSTANT
GOLF LESSONS

GREG NORMAN'S
100
INSTANT
GOLF LESSONS

Greg Norman

with George Peper

ILLUSTRATIONS BY JIM McQUEEN

PELHAM BOOKS

Pelham Books
Penguin Books Australia Ltd
487 Maroondah Highway, PO Box 257
Ringwood, Victoria 3134, Australia
Penguin Books Ltd
Harmondsworth, Middlesex, England
Viking Penguin, A Division of Penguin Books USA Inc.
375 Hudson Street, New York, New York 10014, USA
The Stephen Greene Press Inc.
15 Muzzey Street, Lexington, Massachusetts 02173, USA
Penguin Books Canada Limited
10 Alcorn Avenue, Toronto, Ontario, Canada M4V 3B2
Penguin Books (N.Z.) Ltd
182-190 Wairau Road, Auckland 10, New Zealand

First Published by Penguin Books Australia, 1992
2 4 6 8 10 9 7 5 3 1
Copyright © Great White Shark Enterprises Inc, 1992

Typeset in 13/17 Garamond Euro by Midland Typesetters, Victoria
Made and printed in Australia by Griffin Press

National Library of Australia
Cataloguing-in-Publication data:
Norman, Greg, 1955- .
Greg Norman's 100 instant golf lessons.

ISBN 0 7207 2026 5.

1. Golf . I. Peper, George. II. McQueen, Jim. III. Title. IV.
Title: 100 instant golf lessons. V. Title: Greg Norman's one
hundred instant golf lessons. VI. Title: One hundred instant
golf lessons.

796.3523

To Laura, Morgan Leigh and Gregory

Acknowledgements

My thanks to George Peper for his editorial assistance and to Jim McQueen for the illustrations, which were based upon photographs by Leonard Kamsler.

Conversion

one inch = 2.54 centimetres
one foot = 30.48 centimetres
one yard = 0.91 metre

Contents

Introduction   xi

PART ONE: BEFORE YOU SWING

1	Clap Hands for the Grip	2
2	The Short Thumb	4
3	Look High, Look Low	6
4	Aim the Clubface First	8
5	Your Feet Can Fool You	10
6	Don't Toe the Line	12
7	Posture Is Natural	14
8	The Root of Many Evils	16
9	One Spot for Every Shot	18
10	Suit Yourself	20
11	Get the Picture	22
12	Consider a Bit of Flare	24
13	Open Up on Short Irons	26
14	The Right Height	28
15	Why Jack and I Hover the Club	30
16	A Game of Centimetres	32
17	Get a Countdown	34
18	Step All the Way Back	36

PART TWO: THE LONG GAME

19	Pulling the Trigger	40
20	The Left-elbow Lead	42
21	The Extension Bench	44
22	For Long Drives – R.P.B.	46
23	My Swing Doesn't Change	48
24	Three Wrongs and a Right	50
25	Read Your Wrists	52
26	It's a Horse Race	54
27	Hit the Second Ball	56
28	Tempo and Rhythm	58
29	How to Hit It Off the Deck	60
30	On Long Irons – Don't Try	62
31	For Battles in Britain	64
32	The High Shot	66
33	How to Make It Suck Back	68
34	The Spinless Shot	70
35	Shotmaking Made Easy	72

PART THREE: THE SHORT GAME

36	Throw Yourself Into the Short Game	76
37	They're Just Shorter Swings	78
38	Fit the Swing to the Shot	80
39	Hit Your Short Shots Hard	82
40	One of the Few Laws	84
41	Master the Method, Vary the Clubs	86
42	Chipmaking	88
43	Blast from Bermuda, Putt the Rest	90
44	Deaden Impact with a Putter Grip	92
45	How to Miss It Close	94
46	The Knockdown Punch	96
47	The 7-Fingered Shot	98

48 Don't Be Afraid of This One   100

49 Putters Aren't Just for Putting   102

50 Why You Should Putt Aggressively   104

51 I'm an Apex Putter   106

52 Trust Your Technique   108

53 Keep Your Eye on the Back   110

54 Hold the Hold in Putting   112

55 Know the Breaks   114

56 The Ultimate Nerve Test   116

PART FOUR: BUNKERS AND TROUBLE PLAY

57 Four 'Musts' in Bunkers   120

58 It's Just a Splash   122

59 Play Detective   124

60 Double the Distance in Sand   126

61 The Long-distance Runner   128

62 How to Make It Sit   130

63 Take a Stab at Short Shots   132

64 Seve's Softee   134

65 Slice an 8-Iron   136

66 How to Play the Hardest Shot   138

67 The Best Two Hours You Can Spend   140

68 Slash Your Way Out of Jail   142

69 Grass Knowledge   144

70 Debunking Flyers   146

71 How's It Growing?   148

72 The Lazy Lob   150

73 Living with Divots   152

74 Go Ahead, Have a Blast   154

75 Lean Against the Slope   156

76 Three Tips for Playing in Rain   158

77 Into a Hard Wind, Take a Light Grip   160

78 Don't Fight Crosswinds   162

PART FIVE: MANAGING YOURSELF AND YOUR GAME

79	Know Thyself	166
80	Pace Yourself	168
81	Get the Stiffest Shaft You Can Handle	170
82	Be Bold with Your Strengths	172
83	Pep Talks	174
84	Go to the Movies	176
85	Why I See the Apex	178
86	Suit Your Shot to a Tee	180
87	The Secret Weapon	182
88	Look for 'Bad' Lies	184
89	Play the Hole Backward	186
90	On a Tight Tee Shot, Get Loose	188
91	Walk Smartly	190
92	3-Way Yardage	192
93	Yardage Is Only the Beginning	194
94	Between Clubs, Go with Your Tendency	196
95	Gauging the Greens	198
96	Don't Be a Sucker	200
97	Read Greens from Afar	202
98	My Practice Practices	204
99	Have a Post-round Agenda	206
100	Shake It Off	208

Introduction

It was a pair of instruction books by Jack Nicklaus that launched my education as a golfer. *Golf My Way* presented Jack's overall theory on how to play the game while *My 55 Ways to Lower Your Score* offered quick tips on specific subjects. Jack said that the books were a way for him to give something back to the game that had been so good to him.

Believe me, no one appreciated those gifts more than I did, and a generation later it has been my privilege to be able to pass along some of the things I've learned during my two decades of playing competitive golf around the world.

My earlier book, *Shark Attack!* (Simon & Schuster, 1988) was analogous to *Golf My Way*, a manifesto on how I approach and play the game. The book you're now holding is similar to *55 Ways*. In these pages are one hundred mini-lessons, on every aspect of the game.

These are the lessons I've learned from playing with the world's finest golfers, from listening to the game's top teachers, and most of all from my own experience: pressure-packed tournaments, friendly practice rounds, and lonely sessions on the range. Some of the tips focus on the basics, the simple fundamentals that can't be overstressed; others deal with advanced shots or techniques that will require some practice before you master them. Not every lesson will be useful to you, but with one hundred here for your considera-tion I hope you'll find a few worth trying, and if one or two of them help you take a few strokes off your handicap, then I'll consider this book a success.

Good luck to you, mate.

Greg Norman

PART ONE: BEFORE YOU SWING

Clap Hands for the Grip

I'm not an advocate of any one style of grip. Basically, I think you should hold the club in a way that's comfortable for you. However, I do believe in one rule, and the best way to test it is by clapping your hands.

Take your stance without a club, allowing your arms to hang naturally. Then bring your hands together, palms flat. In this position, note that your palms are parallel. This is the one 'must' of a sound grip – a palms-parallel position – as it allows the hands to work as one unit instead of fighting each other.

Now assume your usual grip on the club, and then open your hands, straightening out your fingers while continuing to hold the club between your palms. Are your palms parallel? If not, you should work them back into the clap-hands position and reassume your grip.

In an ideal neutral grip, the back of your left hand and the palm of your right will be facing your target. With a slightly weak grip the alignment will be a bit toward the ground, and with a slightly strong grip the hands will tilt a bit toward the sky. Neither of these is necessarily bad, as long as the palms are parallel.

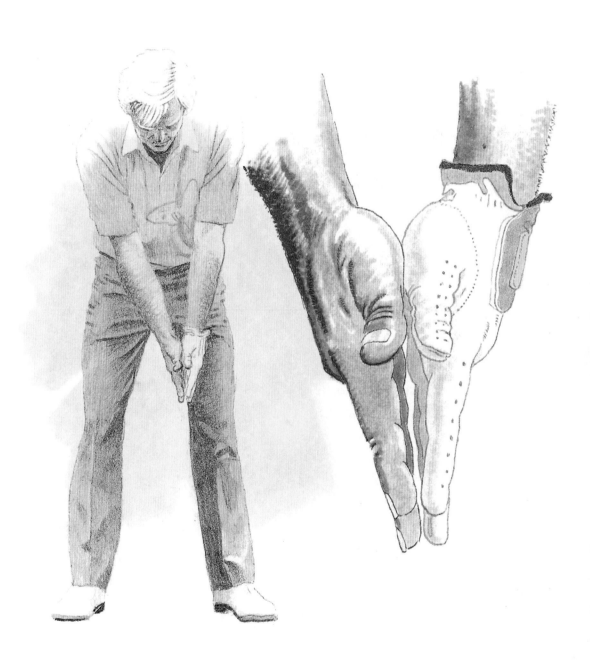

2

The Short Thumb

Proper grip pressure is one of golf's most elusive fundamentals – and it's as difficult to describe as it is to achieve. One method that has helped me set the proper pressure in my left hand is the 'short-thumb' technique.

Take your usual grip on the club, with your left thumb extended straight down the shaft. Now, slide the thumb upward, about a centimetre. Notice the effect this has on the tightness of the hold in the last two fingers of your hand. This is exactly where you want a firm, secure grip.

This is one key that I check all the time. If you occasionally experience a looseness in your swing – or the inaccuracy it causes – I recommend that you too experiment with the short thumb.

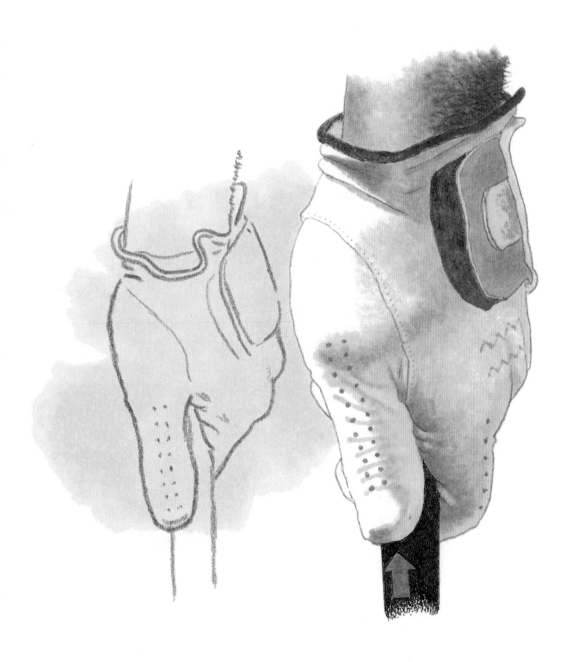

3

Look High, Look Low

Traditional golf instruction tells you to peer straight out at your target and then align yourself with it. Well it may surprise you that when I set up for a shot I sometimes don't even look at the flag. Instead, I look above and below.

Above, to the highest point on the horizon, be it a treetop, a mountain top, or a guy in a red hat standing in the gallery behind the green. Remember, not every shot is played directly at the flag, so it's a good idea to find something that will hold your concentration. Just as important, I find it easier to fix my eyes and mind on specific objects. After all, every flag looks the same.

Then I go below, and seek out an area of the turf just in front of me – a leaf, a discoloured area of grass, a divot – that is directly in line with my earlier, lofty aim spot. This is a technique I learnt directly from a Jack Nicklaus instruction book, and of all the things I've tried to emulate from Jack, it may be the most important. To this day, I can think of no player who consistently aligns himself more accurately than Nicklaus.

4

Aim the Clubface First

Accurate alignment would be a simple matter if we could stand directly on the line that extends from our ball to the target. But the fact is that we stand to the side of the ball, and that makes alignment tough. For this reason, I don't even try to align my body to the target until after I have aligned my clubface. Holding the club in my right hand only, I approach the ball from behind. While I do this, I sight up and down the line that extends from the ball to my target, looking for a spot a few yards in front of my ball and on that line. Once I find that, I set the clubface behind the ball, and swivel it minutely back and forth until it is pointing directly at the spot.

Only after the clubface is squarely in position do I assume my grip and align my body in the address position.

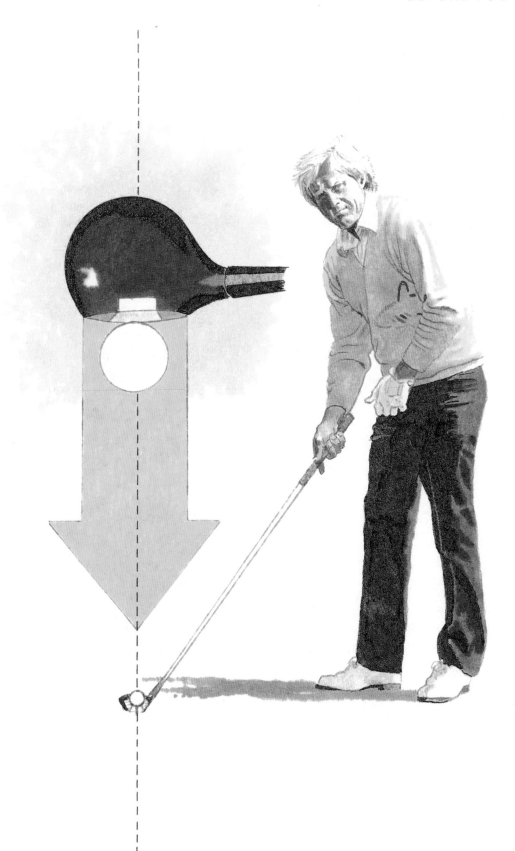

5

Your Feet Can Fool You

One of the most common mistakes I see among my pro-am partners is over attention to the alignment of the feet. They take great pains to set their feet properly while neglecting the position of their hips and shoulders. The fact is, it's easy to look and feel square to the ball while in reality being in a markedly closed or open position. Often, the player initially sets his hips and shoulders just as accurately as his feet, but in the process of waggling and getting comfortable over the ball, he twists his body out of the square position, usually into a more open alignment.

So don't be fooled by your feet. Ask one of your friends to take a critical look at your address position, and if you're out of alignment, tell him to turn your shoulders until you're where you ought to be. Alternatively, take a club, set it across the front of your shoulders, and see where it points. If it's off, realign yourself until the club points parallel to the line connecting your toes. Chances are, this new alignment will feel uncomfortable, but it will be the beginning of straighter, more consistent shots.

Don't Toe the Line

I can't tell you how many times I've seen players – both pros and amateurs – check their alignment by setting a club along the line that connects their toes. In my view, that's a mistake. The reason is that most players tend to flare open one or both of their feet. Most common is the flared left foot, which brings the left toe back four or five centimetres from the target line. The result is that, if you lay a club down from toe to toe, that line will point well left of target, and will not reflect your actual alignment. Your hips, knees, and shoulders may be perfectly square, but the flared toe line will make you look open.

A more precise way to check alignment is to lay the club along your heel line. As your toes flare, your heels remain on line, so the line that connects your heels will accurately reflect the actual alignment of your feet.

Posture Is Natural

There's no need to agonize over getting the 'ideal' position at address. Here's a simple way to find it. Without a club in your hand, flex your knees, bend slightly from the waist, and then let your arms drop down naturally. Clap your hands together, and you'll be in the proper address posture. It's as simple as that. If you grip your club – any club – from this position, you should find that its sole lies flat on the ground. If it doesn't, don't change your posture, change the club.

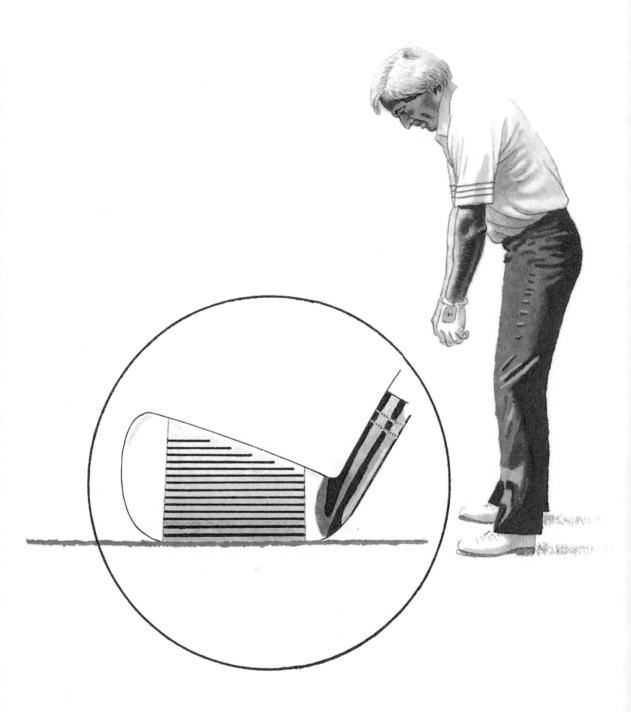

The Root of Many Evils

Invariably, when I find myself hitting a lot of bad shots, the root cause is ball position. Let's say I've had a day when I've pushed a lot of shots to the right. Usually, that means I've let the ball slip too far back in my stance, with the result that my hips and shoulders have rotated a few degrees closed at address. This causes me to hit into the ball slightly more from the inside than usual, resulting in shots that launch to the right of my target.

After a day like that, the first item on my agenda on the practice tee will be to check my ball position. I'll begin by over-compensating – playing the ball way forward, up off my left toe. This will open my stance and cause me to hit the ball from outside to in, producing a bunch of pulled shots and slices. Gradually, I'll move the ball back in my stance, perhaps a half ball back at a time, until the pulls and slices stop and I get a series of straight shots.

If you're serious about playing good golf consistently, I recommend that you consider this type of post-round diagnosis and practice-tee cure, with ball position as your first priority. Once you find the position you like, take careful note of it and make it the first thing you check at address when you play your next round.

One Spot for Every Shot

When it comes to the fundamentals, consistency is paramount. If you can repeat the same positions, moves, and methods over and over, you'll simplify your technique and ingrain the correct habits.

That's one of the reasons why I maintain one ball position for all shots. Then, to make the setup comfortable and the stance stable, I move my *right* foot closer to my left as the loft of the club increases. I realize that many instructors advocate that you move the ball progressively back in the stance as your club shortens. But when you do that, you're changing the loft on the clubs – if you play the 6-iron a bit farther back than the 5-iron, then you're delofting that 6-iron so that it's effectively a short 5-iron. You're also changing the point at which your swing makes contact with the ball. I have enough trouble maintaining one impact point – I don't want to have to deal with a dozen of them.

Unless I'm trying to play a special shot of some sort, I position the ball at a point just back of my left heel. Your own position may be a bit farther forward or back, but I encourage you to determine exactly where it is, and then stick with it for every club in your bag.

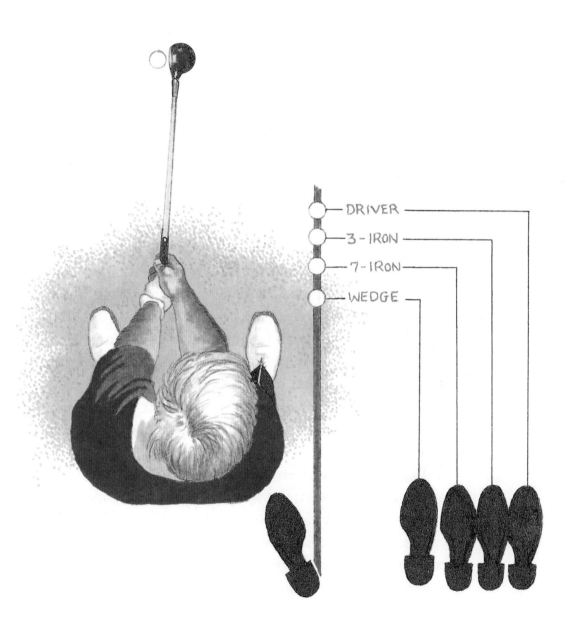

DRIVER

3 - IRON

7 - IRON

WEDGE

10

Suit Yourself

There is no such thing as the 'ideal' ball position. What works for me may not work for you. You might be able to position your ball at least one ball-width forward of where I do and up to two ball-widths farther back.

For each individual, the optimum ball position is at the very bottom of the swing arc. For a short, stout person with a flattish swing arc, that position will likely be relatively far back in the stance. A tall person will have a higher centre of gravity and swing with more lateral movement, which will mean a more forward position. But just as important as your height is how 'leggy' your swing is. Players with active leg action, such as Lee Trevino, should play the ball more forward than those with quieter legs and an active upper body, who tend to trap the ball at an earlier point in the swing in the manner of Arnold Palmer.

The ultimate answer, however, is that your ideal ball position is the spot from which you play your best golf. You owe it to yourself, when you're striking the ball with crispness and consistency, to take careful note of the position of the ball in your stance.

Get the Picture

Once you determine your optimum ball position, the way to preserve it is to take a 'picture' of it.

Set up for a shot, and take careful note of the view you have through your hands to the ball. For me this picture shows the back of my left thumb pad covering the arch of my left foot. When I see the picture, I know I'm in correct alignment and my ball is in its proper position. If I don't see it, I adjust my alignment and/or ball position until I do see that thumb pad eclipsing my instep.

Since I play virtually all my shots from a square stance and with the ball in the same place, this is the picture I always want to see. It stays the same because, as the shaft of the club shortens, my stance narrows slightly, my right foot getting progressively closer to my left as my left foot remains fixed. (See the illustration for Lesson 9.)

Try to fix a similar picture in your mind. It's a great way to add consistency and confidence to your pre-shot routine.

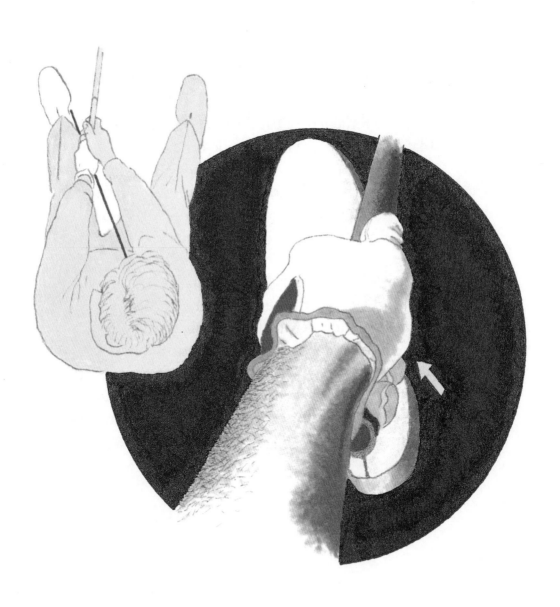

12

Consider a Bit of Flare

At address, my right foot points perpendicular to the target line, but my left foot flares out almost thirty degrees to the left. That's a lot. The reason I do this is that it helps me get my left side out of the way and turn fully through impact. The flip side of this is that the flared-out left toe restricts my hip turn away from the ball and thus limits the length of my backswing. That's not a liability for me, however, because I've been blessed with a supple body.

If you have trouble turning through the ball, I recommend that you experiment with this flared left toe. Just be careful not to allow the alignment of your feet, hips, and shoulders to open (see Lesson 6).

Conversely, if you want to make a more full and free turn on your backswing, try experimenting with a flared right toe. Just bear in mind that this can inhibit your turn through impact.

13

Open Up on Short Irons

Ben Hogan had the right attitude on short-iron shots. He said, 'I want to be known as the man who hit them the straightest, not the longest.'

The 8-iron, 9-iron, and wedges are the control clubs, after all, so there's no point in trying to slug them. I do give these irons a full swing, but I enhance my control with an important change at address. Whereas I address the longer clubs in a square stance – my feet, knees, hips, and shoulders aligned parallel to a line extending from my ball to my target – on the short irons, I open things up a bit. I pull my left foot back a few centimetres from that parallel line, thus rotating my hips, knees, and shoulders a few degrees counterclockwise so that I'm aligned a bit to the left of my target.

This stance facilitates a more upright backswing and a more descending attack on the ball which, on the 8-iron, 9-iron, and wedges, will encourage a straight or softly left-to-right shot with a high, soft trajectory yet lots of backspin on landing.

The Right Height

The traditional advice has been that you should tee your ball so that its equator is even with the top of your driver. These days, that's too simplistic. Metal woods, which are now used by nearly 90 per cent of golfers, have a lower centre of gravity than wood-headed clubs, which means you'll usually want to tee the ball a bit below the 'equator' guideline.

Tee height also depends to some degree on the nature of your swing. If you're a sweeper of the ball you probably prefer a slightly high tee, to give you the feeling of staying behind and under the ball. A more downward hitter, on the other hand, will generally opt for a slightly lower tee to encourage the strong lateral move to the left that creates the down-and-through type of impact.

It's fine to begin with the equator rule, but you may be cheating yourself if you don't experiment a bit with higher and lower tees until you pinpoint the ideal height for your swing and your club.

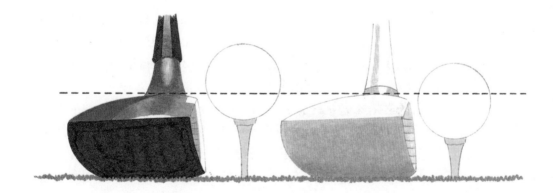

15

Why Jack and I Hover the Club

Early in my golf life I adopted Jack Nicklaus's technique of addressing the ball with the clubhead held just above the turf rather than resting on it. I like the idea for two big reasons.

First, it keeps my grip pressure constant. As you stand over a shot, you have a natural tendency to regrip, and each time your hands shift on the club – even a fraction – it has a major effect on the outcome of the shot. Second, it promotes a very smooth one-piece takeaway with the clubhead flowing straight from the ball. This is particularly true with the driver; there will be no tendency to snap the clubhead up quickly and vertically as there can be when the club is soled.

It's also a valuable technique when your ball is perched in a precarious lie in the rough. Soling the club in such a lie can set off a chain reaction which could move the ball, incurring a penalty. By hovering the club, you not only eliminate that risk, you reduce the tendency to snag the clubface in the grass, both on the takeaway and on the way down to the ball.

I must admit that not many players – pro or amateur – hover the club at address, probably because this is not an easy method to master. But if you can learn it, you'll give yourself some big advantages over the vast majority of golfers.

16

A Game of Centimetres

A change of a few centimetres or less can make a difference of several metres in the distance of your tee shots. Here are two things to experiment with at address:

1. Tee the ball a centimetre higher than normal, about 4 centimetres ahead of your left heel. This will enable you to catch the ball just as your club begins the upswing, which means you'll stay behind the ball longer, allowing an extra split-second to build up power. It also encourages a higher-than-normal shot with plenty of hand time, making this a good ploy when you're hitting with a tail wind.

2. Widen your stance a few centimetres. This will improve your ability to make a long, low takeaway that will increase the length of your swing arc, enabling you to create more clubhead speed on the downswing. The wider stance also lowers your centre of gravity and creates a lower, more boring trajectory, so this adjustment is particularly useful when you're playing into a headwind.

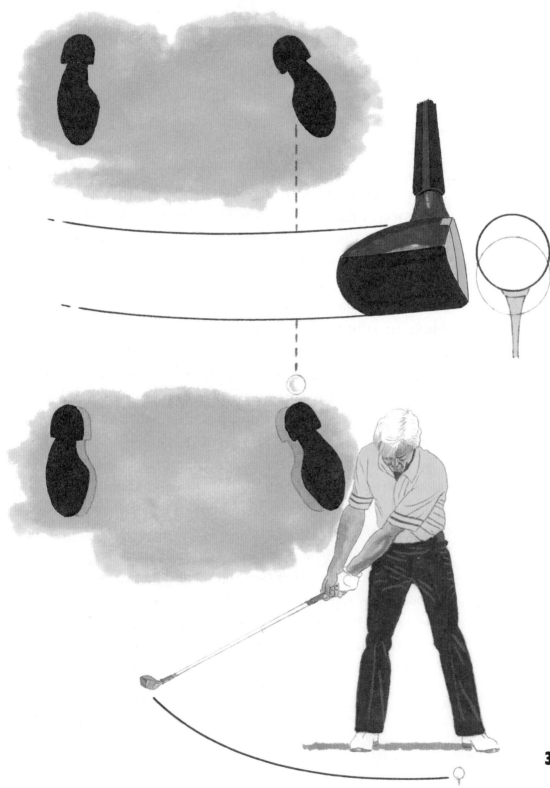

17

Get a Countdown

Recently someone asked me how many times I waggle the club at address. My answer: I have no idea – it may be twice, it may be three times, or more. But I do know that when I'm playing well, it is the same number of waggles for each and every shot I play.

Consistency in your pre-shot routine will breed consistency in your shotmaking. So if you haven't already done so, adopt a 'countdown', a checklist of preparatory movements that begins as you address your ball and ends when you take the club back. My own countdown begins from behind the ball as I get a mental picture of the shot I want to play. Then I step up to the ball, and holding the club in my right hand, I set it down behind the ball, being careful to get the exact alignment. Once that's done, I put my left hand on the club and align my body parallel to the clubface alignment. Then I make those waggles, and I'm set to go.

The reason I can't tell you the number of waggles is that my countdown has become second nature, an almost subconscious, natural continuum that flows directly into the swing. By adopting and ingraining this type of pre-shot routine, you'll keep out negative thoughts and ensure that you're fully focused on the shot at hand.

18

Step All the Way Back

We've all had this experience. You're in the middle of your pre-shot routine – setting your feet, waggling, double-checking your aim – and just as you're about to pull the trigger, a car horn honks. It's even more unsettling when you're standing over a putt.

When that happens, there's only one thing to do. Abort your mission – stop the countdown to impact, and start again from the beginning. Don't just raise up from your crouch over the ball – step all the way back. On occasion, I've gone so far as to actually put the club back in my bag, just so that I could 'take it from the top'. This is the only way to regain the rhythm, comfort, and confidence that are necessary as you prepare to hit any shot.

PART TWO: THE LONG GAME

Pulling the Trigger

For Jack Nicklaus, it's a slight turn of the head. For Gary Player, it's a kicking-in of the right knee. Every good golfer has one, and any golfer who wants to be good needs one: a swing trigger.

The swing trigger is that little movement that takes place when your pre-swing countdown is completed and all systems are 'go' to launch your shot. I have a rather unorthodox one. I slide my hands (along with clubface) outward a bit so that the ball, which in my pre-swing routine was positioned off the toe of the club, now is smack behind the sweet spot.

Some instructors recommend that you develop a swing trigger that helps to remedy a chronic fault. For instance, if you tend to fall back off the ball in the swing, trigger your swing by rocking slightly to your left side before taking the club back. This kind of remedial trigger may or may not work. Frankly, I think it's more important to develop something that's comfortable and will always work smoothly into your swing, no matter what sort of fault you may have now or in the future.

So experiment with different moves – a pump of the grip, a tap of the foot, a flex of the knees – and find yourself a trigger that feels right. Then use it to fire your swing.

20

The Left-elbow Lead

On the practice tee, I have a number of checkpoints I go through, particularly when I'm not swinging as well as I'd like. The most important of these relates to the very start of the swing, where I key on my left elbow.

To ensure that my arms and shoulders move away from the ball in one piece, and that everything starts on a straight line back from the ball, I think of controlling the takeaway with a pushing backward of my left elbow. It's as if that elbow pushes the rest of my upper body back and away. This gets me going in good rhythm and helps encourage a full coil of my shoulders and hips at the top of the backswing.

21

The Extension Bench

The extension position – a point halfway through the backswing where the club extends directly away from your target – is an extremely important movement in the swing, as it is here that the length of your swing arc (and thus your power potential) is established. Too many golfers fail to achieve a proper extension when they either cock their wrists too soon on the backswing or pull the club to the inside and around them rather than pointing it straight back.

My caddie, Bruce Edwards, gave me a good tip for working on the extension. It requires a prop, but one that you'll find on many tees – a bench. Take your stance on one side of the bench with your club extending across to the other side. Then practise making a straight-back takeaway of the club, as far back as you comfortably can. The bench will not allow you to pull the club to the inside, so you'll quickly get the feel of how to establish a full, powerful arc.

22

For Long Drives – R.P.B.

I suspect that I'm one of the few players – pro or amateur – who doesn't have a lot of swing thoughts. On most shots, the only thing I tell myself as I take the club back is 'rhythm'. But now and then, when I'm trying to play a special sort of shot, I will call up an image or thought for extra encouragement.

When my mission is to get maximum distance on a tee shot, in order to reach a par five in two, I'll tell myself: 'R.P.B.' Those initials stand for 'right pocket back', a reminder for me to make a full hip turn in which my right front trouser pocket rotates around toward my back as far as possible. When I make this maximum hip turn, my shoulders also turn fully and I finish the backswing with a full coil that unleashes powerfully on the downswing and into the ball. The principle is the same as with a sling shot – the farther you can pull it back, the faster it will snap through, and the longer the shot will fly.

23

My Swing Doesn't Change

Two qualities that I've tried to build into my game are consistency and simplicity. Nowhere is this more true than in the swing itself. Once I'm settled into my address position, I make no conscious swing adjustments. And I make the same swing for every club in the bag. Whereas many players advocate using a progressively shorter and less forceful swing as the length of the club decreases, I swing back to a parallel position whether the club in my hand is a driver, a 3-wood, a 3-iron, a 7-iron, or a wedge (except for pitches or chips).

As the club shortens, your clubhead arc automatically decreases, so there's no need to throttle back on your tempo. Besides, by keeping your swing length consistent you have the confidence that the length of your shots can be controlled solely through your club selection.

24

Three Wrongs and a Right

I'm an advocate of a big golf swing. Go ahead and take the club back past parallel if you want. But do it right. Be aware that there are three bad ways and one good way to make a big swing.

Bad way number one is by loosening your grip at the end of the backswing, and letting the clubhead flop toward the ground. Unless you can perform a miracle and regrip perfectly before impact, this loose grip will produce loose shots. Faulty method number two – probably the most common error – is overbending the left elbow. This adds a hinge to the swing, a hinge that rarely works smoothly. And the third mistake is to toe-dance at the top of your swing, raising up onto the toe of your left foot as you lurch for the sky. From that position, there is no safe return.

The proper way to make a big backswing is with a big turn of the hips and shoulders. It's okay to have a little lift in your left heel, and it's okay to have a bit of flex in your elbow too. But don't overdo either, and by all means keep a firm hold on the club, particularly in the last three fingers of your left hand. But the key is to turn your hips and shoulders so that at the fullest extent of the backswing your back faces your target. If you can't make this 90-degree-plus turn naturally, then try some flexibility exercises – but don't 'cheat' your way to a big swing, as it will only bring big trouble.

25

Read Your Wrists

The position of your hands at the top of the swing usually predicts the type of impact you'll make.

Hooked and pushed shots tend to come from an overly flat position, where the left wrist is bowed, the club shaft points to the left of target, and the clubface points straight up at the sky. Slices and pulls are the most common results of an upright position at the top, where the left wrist is cupped, the shaft points to the right of the target, and the face of the club is aligned almost vertical with the ground.

In the ideal position, the back of your left wrist should be on a straight line with your arm, and the club should point parallel to your target line. Your clubface will be in a square position, pointing roughly on a 45-degree angle toward the sky.

Photos and videotapes can show you which position you're in, or you can ask a friend to check you on the practice tee. The basic idea is to swing to a position in which your hands are directly above the top of your right shoulder. If you get them outside or below the shoulder you're too flat; if they get between the shoulder and your neck, you're too upright.

26

It's a Horse Race

You should think of your swing as a sort of horse race in which every horse not only leaves the gate at the same instant but also reaches the finish line simultaneously in a mass dead heat.

In the takeaway, all your 'horses' – the arms, legs, hips, shoulders, and club – move away from the ball in a unified movement. The first horses to reach the top of the swing are the knees and hips, followed by the shoulders (which in fact have had to rotate twice the distance). The arms, which have to go farther still, come next, followed by a complete cocking of the wrists as the weight of the clubhead – the last horse to reach the turn – gives a final downward tug.

The pack remains in this general formation at the beginning of the downswing. Indeed, even as the wrists and clubhead are completing the turn, the lower body has begun to head for home. The left knee moves laterally toward the target, thereby pulling on the left hip, which in turn pulls the left arm a bit downward. Then the right knee begins to drive toward the target, bringing the shoulders, arms, wrists, and clubhead into the backstretch.

Then, at the last split-second before impact – the stretch run – the race tightens. The wrists and clubhead, which had been lagging behind, suddenly unleash like a slingshot and catch up with the bigger muscles, with all horses hitting the wire at impact. In a good swing, your impact position is a virtual copy of your address.

27

Hit the Second Ball

Extension back and away from the ball on the takeaway is important to set the full, powerful arc of your swing. But just as important is extension through the ball at and after impact, to keep the club on line for a squarely struck, accurate shot.

If you tend to 'quit' at impact, or if your wrists sometimes break down and you pull the club quickly to the inside, then pretend that you're hitting not one ball but two. Imagine a second ball, approximately 50 centimetres forward of the actual ball and on a straight line from the actual ball to your target. Then, try to 'hit' that second ball as well as the real one. This exercise will ensure that you extend your arms and club properly through impact.

28

Tempo and Rhythm

There's no such thing as the perfect tempo. Ideally each of us should adopt a swing speed that is consistent with our overall temperament. Lanny Wadkins swings quickly, but Lanny does everything quickly. Ben Crenshaw is a more deliberate person, and his swing is slow and smooth.

So suit yourself. But whatever tempo you adopt, be sure that you keep it consistent throughout the round. Try not to speed up when the pressure is on. If you find yourself quickening, then consciously slow things down – slow down your walk, your speech, your club selection.

As for rhythm, there is an ideal, but it can't be described in print. It must be absorbed. The best thing to do is go to the practice tee of a PGA Tour event and spend several minutes watching the players with great rhythm, guys like Seve Ballesteros (pictured), Tom Purtzer, Larry Mize, and Nick Faldo. Then walk – don't run – to the course and try to mimic them.

29

How to Hit It Off the Deck

There are a few par fives that only a long hitter can reach in two, and even then that long hitter has to crush two shots back to back. In such situations, I love to hit my driver 'off the deck' (i.e., off the turf) for my second shot.

It's not as tough as it seems, particularly with today's generation of low-profile metal woods. But before you consider this shot, take a hard look at your lie. The ball doesn't have to be in the fairway. Indeed, if you have a tight lie, you may not want to hit it with the driver. But if the ball is sitting up, in either the fairway or light rough, so that at least part of it is higher than the top of your clubface, then you have an opportunity to go for it.

Control is important, so grip down just a hair – this will help ensure against a fat shot. On the other hand, you don't want to swing above the ball and thin it, so put a bit of extra flex in your knees.

The most important element of this swing is a smooth, long takeaway in which you keep the clubhead low to the ground. If you can take the club back this way, you'll have a good chance of returning it smack into the back of the ball for a clean, strong hit. So widen your stance a bit by moving your right foot back (keeping the ball in its usual position in your stance). As you widen your stance in this way, you'll tend to add a bit more weight to your right side so that instead of a 50-50 distribution it will be 60-40 in favour of the right. This adjustment will set you up for that long, low takeaway.

Don't worry about any other adjustments. Simply trust your swing, trust your lie, and trust your driver to do the work. Remember that you have a powerful club in your hand and clean contact is all you want – you don't need to attack the ball. Quite the contrary, on the downswing you should feel as if your upper body is hanging back as your legs drive through impact. If you can stay behind this ball, you'll have the best chance of pushing it forward.

30

On Long Irons – Don't Try

If there's one area of the game that separates good golfers from middle and high handicappers, it's the ability to play long-iron shots.

I won't kid you that these are the easiest clubs in the bag. On the other hand, they aren't as difficult to master as most people think. The best advice I can give you is one of philosophy: Don't try too hard. Amateurs watch the pros hit long, high, arcing 2-irons and then they go out and try to make their own 2-irons do the same thing.

But the key is not to make it happen but to let it happen. Don't try to hit the ball hard or high. In fact, don't try to hit the ball at all – just make a smooth swing at it. Pretend the club in your hand is a 7-iron and the distance you have is 7-iron distance. Then swing that '7-iron' in the same confident way you always do. Think of the ball as merely a point on the path of your swing.

31

For Battles in Britain

Modern golf courses usually call for target golf, where you loft your shots like darts from toe to fairway and fairway to green. But if you've ever travelled to the courses of Great Britain, or if you play much of your golf in the wind, you're well aware of the value of a low shot.

I think of it as a long punch shot. The key is to push the ball outward on a low trajectory rather than lofting it into the air. You can pre-programme this effect at address by setting up with the ball a bit back, just in back of your left heel. The majority of your weight should be on your left side, but you should not put so much weight there that you fall ahead of the ball as you get to impact.

I also find that a good way to keep the ball low is to keep my body low during the swing, so I squat down a bit at address. The swing should be controlled, and your backswing should probably not go beyond the three-quarter point. But the key is in the takeaway, which should be as long and low as possible. If you take the club back very low, then you will return it to the ball that way, and it is that shallow angle of attack that will keep the ball low.

32

The High Shot

One of the hardest things for many amateur players to do is to hit the ball high into the air. One reason is the contrary nature of golf – if you try to hit up on a ball, you'll usually top it. So do yourself a favour and make no changes in your swing. Just make two minor adjustments in your stance. First, play the ball slightly forward of its normal position. If you usually position it off your left instep, move it about a ball-width forward, off your left instep. Assuming that your normal ball position allows you to hit the ball at the bottom of your downswing, the forward position will ensure that you'll catch it at the beginning of your upswing.

Second, redistribute your weight at address, so that you feel a bit more weight on your right side. This will shift your centre of gravity – and your swing centre – behind the ball a bit, which is where it needs to be at impact if you want to achieve a high trajectory.

Then just make a normal swing, the goal of which should be to finish with your hands high. Don't feel as if you have to chase after the ball because it's forward in your stance, and above all, don't try to hit up on the ball. With the changes you've made at address, you'll do that naturally.

33

How to Make It Suck Back

One of the most dramatic things anyone can do to a golf ball is apply so much backspin that, after landing, it sucks backward as if on a string. In addition to being fun to watch, this is a useful shot, especially when you're playing to rock-hard greens or when you need to get close to a pin that is positioned just beyond a bunker or other trouble.

In order to play this shot successfully, you need to have several factors in your favour, only one of which is the proper swing. The first essential is a clean lie, to enable maximum application of clubface to ball. It also helps to be playing into the wind and to a green that slopes toward you. Finally, your chances of applying backspin will be enhanced if you're playing with square-grooved irons and striking a soft-covered ball.

The key to the technique is to make crisp, brisk impact with the back of the ball. Ideally, in fact, you want to hit the top-back quadrant of the ball, so that you squeeze the ball against the turf for a millisecond. That's what creates the friction that makes the ball spin.

Begin by positioning the ball a few centimetres or so back of its usual position in your stance. Don't move it any farther back, because that will simply produce a low, squirting shot. Grip the club more firmly than normal, to reduce wrist action – you want hand speed but not wrist speed.

The swing should be aggressive from top to bottom.

Contrary to common belief, the suck-back shot is played with the big muscles – it is not a flick. Keeping those wrists firm, swing through briskly with the arms as your legs and lower body move toward the target.

You don't want to pick this ball cleanly, but you don't want a divot either. You'll know you've played it well when at impact you slick down the grass in front of the ball.

34

The Spinless Shot

I'm known as a player who puts a lot of backspin on the ball, but the fact is, I also know how to hit a shot that has almost no spin. This is a handy shot to have, particularly when you want the ball to sort of thud down and stop on the green.

Outwardly the swing for this shot looks much the same as that for any other iron shot. Your ball position should be a bit more forward – perhaps a half ball – than usual, but the big difference is in the way you feel during the swing. It's a loose and 'oily' feeling to borrow one of Sam Snead's words. Whereas on most shots you maintain a certain amount of tension in your legs, for this shot you unlock those muscles in your thighs and calves so that your swing flows with extra smoothness. Your knees don't fire as they do on other swings, and your leg action is soft and yielding. At impact, your club clips the ball with a 3-wood-like angle of attack, rather than the more downward blow that takes a divot.

35

Shotmaking Made Easy

For the most part, I'm a straight-ball hitter. I don't try to play a lot of fancy shots from right to left and from left to right. And when I do work the ball, I keep the method simple. Making no changes in grip or swing, I set up fades and draws entirely with my alignment at address.

For a left-to-right fade I align my body slightly to the left while keeping my clubface aimed straight at the target. By pointing my toe line, knees, hips, and shoulders to the left, I set up an out-to-in cut across the ball, which imparts the clockwise sidespin that makes the ball drift to the right.

Conversely, for a right-to-left draw I aim my body to the right while keeping the clubface straight at the target. This alignment encourages a takeaway that is more to the inside than usual, resulting in a more in-to-out hit on the ball; this counterclockwise spin moves shots from right to left.

The more curve I want on these shots, the more I open or close my stance. It's as simple as that.

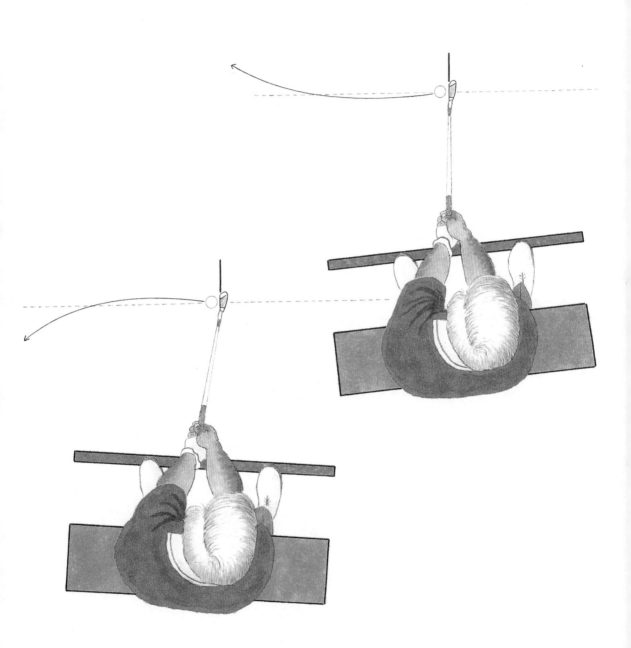

PART THREE: THE SHORT GAME

36

Throw Yourself Into the Short Game

For years, I played the pro circuit without having a feel for the short game. Then one day, I turned things around – not by hitting balls but by tossing them.

For an entire day I tossed golf balls, from a variety of positions and to a variety of targets. I must have tossed over 500 of them, carefully noting the way each ball reacted after it hit the green. That was the day I learned the meaning of touch.

I recommend this exercise to you, whether you have a good short game or not. Take a dozen or so balls and toss them, underhanded, all toward the same target. Cup each ball in the palm of your hand and toss it with a stiff-wristed motion. This will give you a feel for the properly firm wrist action in chipping.

Toss high balls that fly all the way to the hole and sit, and others that roll almost like putts. Make some downhill and uphill tosses as well, to see which type trajectory and roll works best in which situations. I suspect you'll find, as I did, that the 'low road' is easiest to regulate, whether you're tossing a ball with your hand or chipping it with a golf club. Above all, however, you'll gain an understanding of the intricacies of the short game, where imagination and innovation are paramount.

37

They're Just Shorter Swings

There are all sorts of theories regarding the way to hit pitch and chip shots. Ken Venturi, a fine teacher, advocates an absolutely stiff-wristed technique. Phil Rodgers, another excellent teacher, professes an extremely wristy method.

Frankly, I think both of them are making things too complicated. To my mind, the pitch and chip are simply small golf swings. Your stance, which narrows from the driver to the short irons, narrows still further for the pitch and chip, and also continues to open up as on the short-iron shots, to the point that on a chip shot your heels are no more than 15 to 20 centimetres apart and you're aligned about 20 degrees left of your target. Your ball position remains the same as for all your shots, somewhere off the left heel to the instep for most people.

From a compact stance, you simply make a proportionately compact swing at the ball. Wrist action is neither restricted nor forced – it's as natural as in a full swing, the result of a swinging back of the arms.

38

Fit the Swing to the Shot

One of the trickiest parts of the short game is the matter of adjusting the distance of your pitch shots. Let's say you face a 70-metre pitch on one hole and a 60-metre pitch on the next. How do you take those 10 metres off the shot?

Some instructors advocate varying the force of the swing. I'm dead against that. Except on special shots such as the lob and the punch, I'm a strong believer in keeping the pace and tempo of the swing absolutely consistent.

Instead, I prefer to vary the length of the swing. Contrary to my method in the long game, where I play all full shots with the same length of swing, I shorten my backswing as the length of my pitch shot decreases. Furthermore, as I get closer to the green, I also grip down on the club, right down to the metal on pitches of only a few metres. This enables me to make a firm, aggressive, accelerating swing, which maintains a firm and confident attack on the ball.

Inside 30 metres or so, I simplify things even more by switching from a pitching wedge to a sand wedge while maintaining the same technique I use for longer pitches. If you carry a third wedge, you can take this system a step further. After all, why grip way, way down and make a tiny swing when there's a club in your bag that will do the work for you?

39

Hit Your Short Shots Hard

Have you ever watched Tom Watson play chips and pitches around the green? If you haven't you should, because he is just about the best there is. One quality you'll notice is that although the shots he's hitting are short ones, he hits them hard, with a brisk, compact, up-and-down stroke.

Acceleration through impact is as vital to the short game as it is with your longer irons and woods. It is the only way to put proper backspin on these shots, for maximum control. So be crisp and aggressive on even your shortest shot, leading the clubhead with your hands as you make a descending hit on the ball. One way to check yourself is to imagine the short-shot swing as a race between your hand and the clubhead, with your left knee as the finish line. If your hands don't win that race every time, you need to develop a faster, harder-hitting technique.

40

One of the Few Laws

Chipping is a bit like putting – it's built around feel and confidence – and if you can find a method that works for you, you should stick with it, no matter how strange it may seem.

Still, there are a few undeniable laws of the short game, and one of them is to grip down on the club. Once I'm within about 50 metres of the hole, I start choking down on my grip. The shorter the shot I'm facing, the shorter the grip I take – sometimes right down to the metal – and for two reasons. First, it improves touch. By gripping down on the club you put your hands closer to the clubhead and the ball, and that enhances your feel for the shot – it's almost as if you're tossing the ball. Second, by shortening the distance between your hands and the clubhead, you curtail the arc of the swing. This automatically shortens the shot without you having to make big adjustments in your swing length or pace. You can make a crisp, authoritative swing without worrying about hitting the ball well past the pin.

41

Master the Method, Vary the Clubs

Jack Nicklaus likes to hit about 90 per cent of his shots around the green with one club, his sand wedge. He plays it back or forward in his stance and varies his wrist action and swing speed to create several different sorts of chips and pitches.

As much as I admire Jack and agree with his approach to the game, I part company with him on this point. Why work hard at adapting one club to a dozen different situations, when you have at least a half dozen other clubs in your bag to do the work for you, especially if you don't have the talent of Nicklaus?

In most greenside situations, my goal is to get the ball rolling like a putt as soon as possible. I figure I have a better chance of judging and ultimately holing this type of shot than I would if I were to try to loft and spin the ball. Thus, I usually select the club with the least loft possible, given the situation at hand. If I have a chip of less than 7 metres to the flag, I'll usually take a wedge or 9-iron. As the shot gets longer, I'll use the middle irons. On the longest of chips, I'll go down as far as a 5- or 4-iron. In each case, I'll use the same, simple back-and-through chipping motion. By keeping your technique consistent, you reduce the variables and doubts, and encourage a firm, confident swing.

42

Chipmaking

The chip shot is a miniature golf swing, and like the swing it can be altered to play different kinds of shots. By playing the ball back in your stance and using a low takeaway and a horizontal attack on the ball, you can hit sort of a driving chip that rolls a long way; by playing the ball a bit forward in your stance and using more wrist action, you can add trajectory and backspin.

Occasionally, I'll even cut or hook my chips. When I feel my sand wedge will produce a shot with too much height and bite, I'll take a pitching wedge and hit the ball with more of a downward chop than usual; this will impart less loft than on a normal shot with that club but still give me the amount of roll I want. On the other hand, I'll sometimes toe the clubface in and lift the heel of the club off the ground – this will give me a shot that kind of pops out of the ground, still with plenty of loft, but with more roll than I'd get from a traditional chip shot.

There are other sorts of hybrid chips and pitches, but the best way to learn them is through experimentation on your own. Do yourself a big favour and spend an hour or two around the practice green. Put yourself in a bunch of different lies and situations, and then experiment with a variety of ball positions, clubface angles, and degrees of wristiness in your stroke, until you can match each situation with a shot of your own.

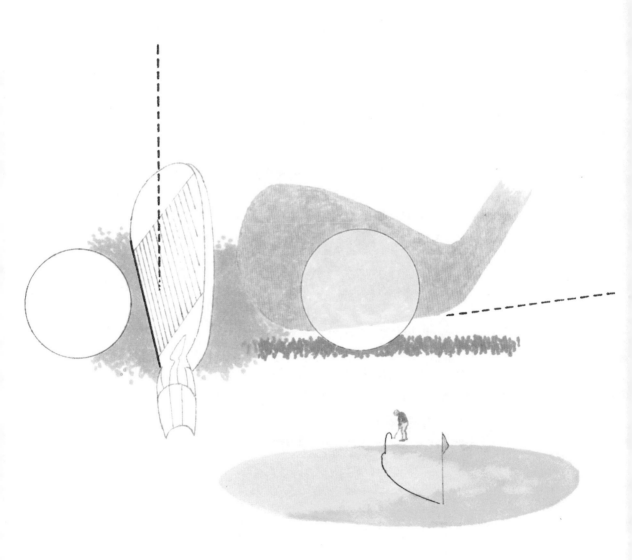

43

Blast from Bermuda, Putt the Rest

Let's say you're just off the green – not in the fringe but just beyond it in slightly thicker grass. You have a shot of about 10 metres. Most people would call it a chip, but I never view it that way. From Bermuda grass, which tends to snatch at your club on a normal chip shot, the best shot is a blast, just as you'd play a ball in a bunker. With an open stance and an open clubface, take a short, upright swing and slide your club – preferably a sand wedge – down into the grass about 2 centimetres behind the ball. The club will slip under the ball and pop it up.

From other kinds of grass, whether in the fringe or in slightly heavier lies, the proper method is almost like a putting stroke – a smooth pendulum-like strike against the back of the ball, to minimize the chance of a sudden acceleration into the ball. You can play this easy shot with anything from an 8-iron to a pitching wedge, regulating the length of a shot simply by changing the length of your backswing, as you would with a putt.

BERMUDA   OTHER

44

Deaden Impact with a Putter Grip

Believe it or not, you can get a 'flyer' to lie within a couple of feet of the green. When the ball sits in the long fringe or rough, half-covered by grass, it will tend to jump out low and fast, without much backspin, just as a full shot does from light rough.

These shots are extremely difficult to control. What you must try to do is deaden impact. I've found that a great way to ensure that is to adopt my putting grip, a reverse overlap in which the index finger of my left hand overlaps the last three fingers of my right. This gives me the same quiet, wristless stroke as on the putting green, and it is that wristless stroke that effectively deadens impact and reduces the flyer effect. Instead of shooting out, the ball pops up softly and lands on the green.

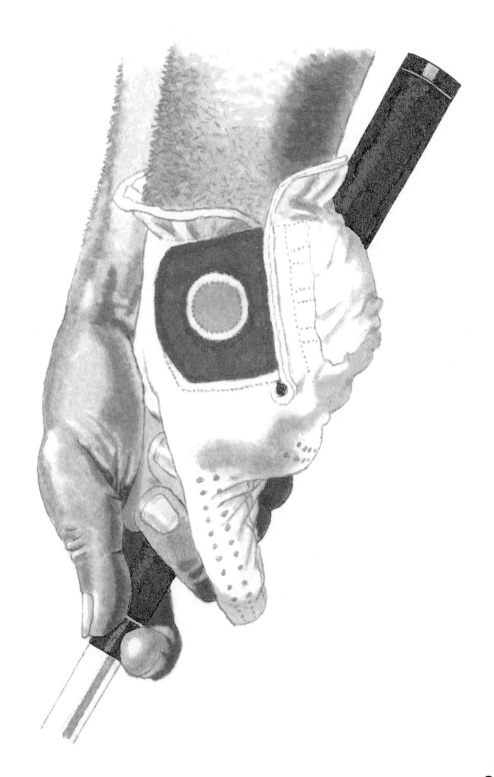

45

How to Miss It Close

We've all experienced the dreaded fat wedge shot, where the clubface digs into the grass behind the ball and the ball goes only a few metres. But did you realize that this 'mistake' is also a legitimate greenside shot?

Consider this situation. You're in the rough and a bunker separates you from the green. Because the ball is sitting down, you know that in order to get it out you'll have to apply such force that the ball will soar clear over the green.

In this predicament, your only shot is the intentional fat shot. You play it the same way as a bunker shot, from a wide-open stance and with a wide-open wedge. What you want to do is slice into the turf with the heel of the wedge. This will open a slit in the ground and the rest of the club will carve under the ball. Hit down hard, and enter the turf about 3 centimetres behind the ball.

The turf will act as a buffer between the club and ball, and the ball will come out as softly as a sand shot. But before you go out and try this in your next match, be aware that two things are absolutely vital: soft turf and hard practice.

46

The Knockdown Punch

The punch shot is not really a shot at all. It's nothing but a long, hard chip. It may be hit with anything from a 6- or 7-iron to a pitching wedge, depending on the length of the shot and whether you want it to run a long way or stop quickly.

The punch is a wise shot to play on holes where you have a wide expanse of firm fairway leading to an open green, as is often the case on the British and Irish courses. But it's probably most useful in a heavy wind, as its low, boring trajectory is less buffeted by the breeze.

The address position is almost the same as for a chip shot. You grip down on the shaft of the club and play the ball back near the centre of your stance, so that your hands are well forward and about two thirds of your weight is on your left side. However, this is one short shot that you may play from a square stance – there's no need to open up your body for a more vital hit, since your object is to hit the ball with a relatively shallow angle of attack.

Another aspect of the punch shot is that it is played with a relatively fast swing, like a boxing jab. It's a quick back-and-through motion with some snap to it. Keep your wrists out of it, and try to keep the club as low to the ground as possible throughout the swing. The follow-through is very short – your hands shouldn't move much past your left knee.

Practise this one on the course a few times if you can,

to get a feel for the distance the ball goes. Yardage is virtually irrelevant on the punch shot – you can punch a wedge 100 metres but you can punch a 6-iron the same distance – so get a feel for the way this shot behaves when hit with each of your clubs.

47

The 7-Fingered Shot

Here's a shot that may sound frighteningly difficult to play but isn't, once you've practised it a couple of times. You use it when you're in the rough near the green and you have to play a high, soft shot that stops quickly after hitting the green. I adapted this technique from the bunker play tip Seve Ballesteros taught me several years ago (see Lesson 64).

Set up just as you would for a little flip shot – open stance, slightly open face on your wedge, weight about 60 per cent on your left side. Then make a swing as you normally would except, just prior to impact, loosen the grip pressure on the last three fingers of your left hand. Don't actually let go of the club, but do lighten the pressure to almost nothing. The result will be that your right hand will take over and will flick the clubhead down, through, and steeply upward. The shot will rise quickly, descend softly, and come down like the proverbial butterfly with sore feet.

48

Don't Be Afraid of This One

Here's a shot that has come into the game only recently – first popularized by Lee Trevino back in the '70s: the sand wedge putt.

Today, almost everyone on the pro circuit uses it – and yet I see very few amateurs giving it a try. That's too bad because it's a very useful shot, and you don't have to have the touch of Trevino to pull it off.

When your ball is in light rough, just off the edge of the green, or is sitting on the outer edge of the fringe with its back up against the rough, you have a unique problem. More often than not, you want to get the ball rolling rather than try a chip. But if you use your putter, the flat blade will have trouble gliding through any grass that's taller than fringe.

That's why pros use the sand wedge, where the sharp, heavy leading edge of the clubface cuts smoothly through the blades of grass. I'll grant you, the flange adds a bit of weight and therefore puts extra power into the hit, and it will take you a bit of practice to get a feel for distances on this shot. But the swingweight of both clubs should be about the same, and you should play it exactly as you would a putt, right down to your putting grip. Try to make that leading edge of the wedge strike the back of the ball. This may mean choking up on the grip a bit, and that's another reason the shot takes a bit of practice. But don't be afraid to try it. Once you're comfortable with it, you'll find it's much less risky than using a putter.

49

Putters Aren't Just for Putting

One of the qualities that separates guys like Seve Ballesteros and Lee Trevino from the rest is an intangible – imagination. Those two not only know how to hit shots, they know how to 'see' them, to look beyond the traditional ways of propelling the ball and invent new methods.

I'm not as creative as Seve and Lee, but I do like to experiment with shots now and then. I surprised a couple of my colleagues in a tournament recently by playing a chip shot with a 5-wood. That's not a shot I'd generally recommend, but I do advocate using your putter in places other than the green.

In the British Open I use it often, bumping the ball down the hard, sparse fairways and up onto the greens. From a good lie on firm sand in a greenside bunker, a putter is often the safest choice, assuming of course that there is no lip to clear. Occasionally, I even use a putter to get the ball out of thick rough around the green.

There are a couple of ways you can strike the ball with it. One is by banging straight down on the ball; this will cause the ball to pop up and out of the grass. Or if you have a putter with a broad, flat toe, you can actually strike the ball with the toe turned sideways (perpendicular to the ball), using the same stroke you would on a putt. It's the same principle as putting with the sand wedge; in heavy grass, a putter turned in this way glides through the grass with less impedance than it would if you were to wield it in the usual manner.

50

Why You Should
Putt Aggressively

Amateur golfers should putt more boldly than pros. In fact, I think you should never lag a putt – you should try to sink every putt you face. For several reasons.

There are only four ways to miss a putt – long, short, left, or right (see illustration A). If you always get the ball to the hole, you eliminate one way. Besides, research has proved that the putt that has the best chance of going in, is one that is struck with sufficient force to carry it 40 centimetres beyond the cup.

Along with this goes the psychological side. Think about the last time you missed several putts in a row by hitting them dead in the jaws of the hole but leaving them just short (see illustration B). Pretty frustrating wasn't it? Such chronic shortness can get to you, whereas hitting the ball consistently past the cup is rarely as unsettling.

Remember that if you hit the ball a bit too hard, you can watch the way it rolls as it passes the hole, getting an immediate read on the return putt, but if you leave it short, you have no such knowledge for the last metre of the putt. Also, on short putts, a bold, firm hit is usually best, as it tends to take the guesswork out of the break in the putt (see illustration C).

Furthermore, a bold stroke is a confident stroke, one with built-in acceleration through impact, a stroke that works on any type of green surface, fast or slow, bent or Bermuda. Aggressiveness on the green is also an asset in match play. Out on the Pro Tour, if we sink a long putt it merely means saving one stroke out of 72 holes. In your weekend Nassau, however, a long putt will invariably win you one of the 18 holes, while having a jarring effect on your opponent (see illustration D).

Finally, and perhaps most important, amateur players can recover from a short drive with a good approach, or from a short approach with a good pitch. But there is no recovery on the putting green. A putt left short is a stroke lost. So don't cheat yourself in the area where you have every capability to be proficient and every reason to be aggressive. Putt boldly.

51

I'm an Apex Putter

One of the biggest putts of my life was the one I sank at Winged Foot on the 72nd hole of the 1984 U.S. Open. Although I lost that championship in an 18-hole play-off with Fuzzy Zoeller, I will never forget the exhilaration of that putt. It was a downhill, twisting 15 metres, and to this day I'm convinced I made it because I tried to hit the ball, not to the hole, but to a point along the path to the hole. There was a slight discolouration in the green about a third of the way to the hole, and when my ball rolled over it, I knew I'd hit the perfect putt.

That's the way I play all my putts. I pick out a point at the very apex of the break, and align myself to that spot. I putt this way for a couple of reasons. The first is that there's no point in thinking past that apex; once I get the ball to that point and with the proper speed, it's on its own. I can't direct the ball past this spot, so I don't see any point in thinking beyond it. Secondly, when one does concentrate on the hole on a breaking putt, there can be a tendency to direct your swing that way as well, resulting in pulls on right-to-left putts and pushes on left-to-rights. When you concentrate on the apex spot, you're immune to this.

52

Trust Your Technique

I putt with the same method today that I used when I began playing golf at age 15. I hold the putter with a reverse overlap grip, stand rather tall to the ball in a slightly open stance, and use a stroke that works like a door opening and closing, similar to Ben Crenshaw's.

I don't necessarily recommend this method to you. Each of us should find a putting technique that suits us. The method I've described works for me.

However, for a period of seven years I abandoned this method. Back in the 1978 British Open at St. Andrews, five-time British Open Champion Peter Thomson told me I'd never be a great putter with the method I had.

So for seven years I tried to change. Those were the worst putting years of my career. And that experience has left me with the conviction that if you have a putting method that works for you, you should never try to fiddle with it. If your stance and stroke feel natural, and if you can get around the course in 31 putts or better consistently, stick with your method. I don't care whether you putt stiff-wristed, flippy-wristed, cross-handed, knock-kneed, or standing on your head. If it works, stick with it.

53

Keep Your Eye on the Back

Bobby Jones likened the putting stroke to driving a tack into the back of the ball. I've always thought that was a good image. However, it was probably more useful in Jones's era than it is today. Back then, the greens were a lot thicker and slower, and the ideal stroke was a forceful, aggressive pop through the ball. But on the close-cut superfast greens we play today, smoothness and control are the keys. Driving a tack may suggest too vigorous a hit.

Still, the notion of bringing the putter into the back of the ball is, I think, an important one. That's why when I putt I don't just look at the whole ball, I look at the back of the ball. By focusing on the back, you help ensure that you'll strike the ball from straight behind it, which in turn will encourage you to make the proper low back-and-through stroke. It is only this type of stroke that imparts a true roll to the ball.

54

Hold the Hold in Putting

Putting feel is a mysterious and elusive thing. You can have great touch on the first green and lose it by the second, unexplainably. You can also have it on the practice stroke but lose it by the time you strike the ball. But in that case, I have an explanation.

Most players – even most Tour pros – loosen their grip on the club after their practice stroke, then regrip as they settle in for the actual stroke. I think that's a bad idea. I prefer to do what Ray Floyd, Tom Watson, and a few others do – hold the hold. From the time I take my practice stroke to the time I hit the ball, my hands do not budge on the club. This is contrary to my routine on every other golf shot, where a certain amount of grip adjusting and 'pumping' take place as I settle in over the shot.

The key is to make your practice stroke more than a wave of the putter. It should be a dress rehearsal for the swing, using exactly the same length and force of swing that you want to apply to the actual stroke. Then, maintain that hold on the putter and step into the real thing. The swing feel will still be in your hands.

55

Know the Breaks

The amount of break you should read into a putt varies not simply with the degree of slope but according to a number of other factors as well. Perhaps most important, Bermuda grass greens break more than greens of rye or bentgrass.

However, no matter what sort of grass you're playing on, you should allow for more break under each of the following situations: (1) on a hard-surfaced green, (2) in dry, sunny conditions, (3) when the grain of the green grows in the same direction as the slope, (4) when putting downhill, and (5) when you're putting straight downwind or a crosswind is blowing down the slope of the green. In each of these situations, the speed of the putt will be increased, calling for a softer, more slowly rolling putt that will be more influenced by the various factors.

Conversely, you should play for less break when (1) on a soft-surfaced green, (2) in rainy conditions on a wet green, (3) the grain of the green grows in the opposite direction of the slope, (4) putting uphill, and (5) you're putting into a headwind or when a crosswind is blowing against the pitch of the slope. These conditions call for a putt that must be struck more firmly, and when you do that, you always play less break.

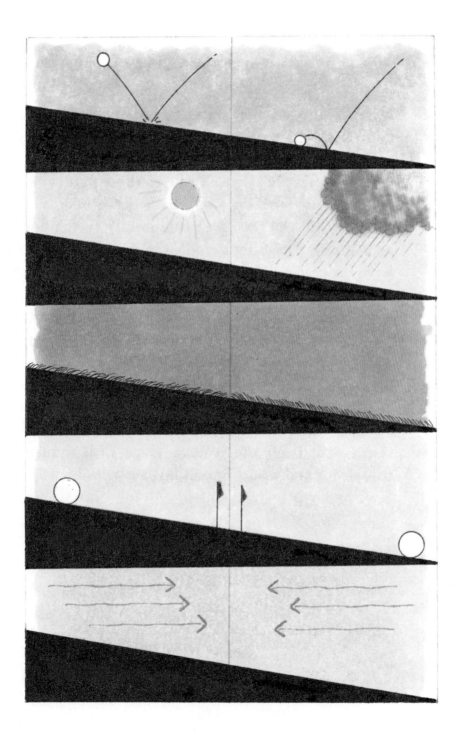

56

The Ultimate Nerve Test

I practise hitting short putts, not to hone my technique but to hone my nerves. I do this through a practice game which I recommend to you.

It's very simple. Try to make 25 short putts in a row. Start with two-footers – and that's not as easy as it may sound. When you get close to number 25, the tension will be palpable, especially if you've made a promise not to leave the practice green until you've made 25 in a row.

Once you've made all the two-footers, move up to three-footers (and plan to be out on the green for a while). When I have an all-out practice session, I'll also go on to four-footers, and on rare occasions I'll even get as far as the five- and six-footers. (Note: 2 metres = 6 feet approximately). I've made 25 consecutive six-footers only a couple of times in my life, but on those occasions, I can assure you, I left the practice green with tremendous confidence in my putting and my nerves.

PART FOUR: BUNKERS AND TROUBLE PLAY

57

Four 'Musts' in Bunkers

Good bunker technique boils down to four keys:

1. Get good footing: By grinding your feet firmly into the sand you'll get a solid, secure base for optimum balance.

2. Grip down a few centimetres on the club: Do this to compensate for the fact that you've ground your feet into the bunker, thus bringing your hands closer to the ball. If you don't shorten your grip, you'll tend to dig the club in too deeply.

3. Open your stance: Set up with your feet, knees, hips, and shoulders pointing well left of your target. This will facilitate the steeply upward takeaway and downward impact that are vital for 99 per cent of greenside bunker shots.

4. Don't keep your eye on the ball: Instead, focus on a point about two centimetres or so behind the ball. That is where you want to make impact.

58

It's Just a Splash

If you understand the physics of impact in a bunker, you'll have a feel for how to play some of the specialized shots.

It's the same as splashing in a pool. If you want to create a high, short splash, you slap sharply down and into the water. If you want a longer, lower splash, you whisk your palm across the surface in a skimming motion.

Imagine a golf ball riding on the crest of those waves, and you'll understand what's at work in bunker play. For a short, high shot, you must hit down sharply, and for a longer shot, your angle of attack must be more lateral.

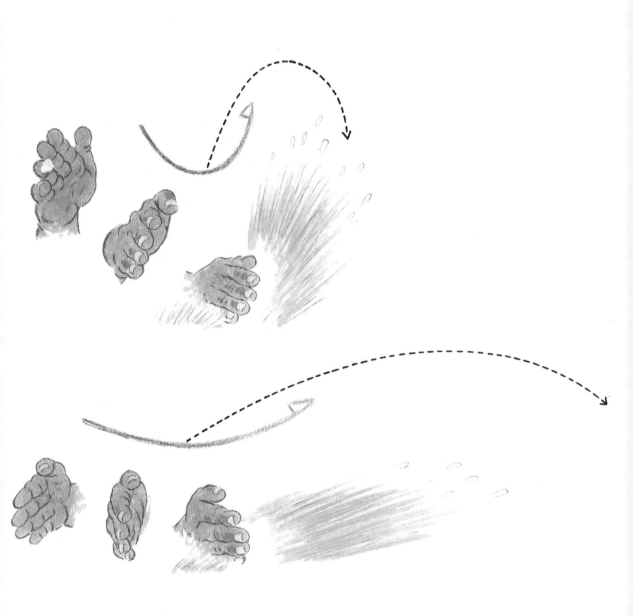

Play Detective

As you walk into a bunker, don't just look at your lie – use your feet to get a feel for the sand. How soft is it, and how deep do your feet sink before hitting the firm base of sand? Pay particular attention to the area immediately behind your ball. Often when you see a Tour pro hit a sand shot that flies well past the pin, and then see him look quizzically down at the sand, what has happened is that the sand under his ball was less deep than it was in the area of his stance. He probably made a good swing for the lie he thought he had. So as you settle in over the ball, grind your spikes into the sand, both to get a firm footing and to get a feel for the sand in the vicinity of your ball.

Take note of the condition of the sand. If recent rain has compacted it, you won't have to hit the ball as hard as if the sand is dry and fluffy. Sometimes you can get a hint at the sand softness by taking a close look at the lie of your ball. If it's sitting completely atop the sand and has left no track in rolling to its lie, then you're on hard, probably crusty sand that won't require a hard swing. If the ball is sitting down and has produced a bit of a trough before coming to rest, the sand is probably soft and you'll have to put a bit of extra force into your swing.

Double the Distance in Sand

Generally speaking, I don't like playing golf according to numbers, but there's one formula that seems to work pretty well. When you're in a bunker, and not buried, swing at the ball with about the same force you'd use for a fairway shot of twice the distance. In other words, for a standard bunker shot of 6 metres imagine that you have a pitch shot of 12 metres.

The Long-distance Runner

When I'm in the sand and have plenty of room between me and the pin, I like to let the ball run most of the way – that's much easier and safer than trying to explode it all the way to the cup on the fly.

For this shot I position the ball about midway between my feet. The clubface is open and laid back, which means it's pointing about a metre right of my target and the face is angled almost toward the sky. This address sets me up for a markedly upward backswing, which I emphasize by breaking my wrists quickly. It's not a long swing – my hands don't go beyond shoulder height – but I do swing forcefully down and through to a full finish. The ball comes out quickly and with almost no spin. I usually try to fly it about a third of the way to the hole and let it run from there.

62

How to Make It Sit

Most average golfers would love to know how to play that sand shot that takes one bounce and then stops dead. Well, here's how I do it.

I start with the open stance and open, laid-back clubface just as for the running shot. (The higher the lip I have to clear, the more open and laid back the clubface is.) But the difference is that I play the ball forward in my stance, up off my left instep. This enables me to hit the shot more on the upswing, lifting the ball on a rising wave of sand.

Just before the swing, I tell myself, 'Slow back, slow through,' because smooth tempo is important on this one. If you've watched the Tour pros on TV carefully, you've noticed how slowly they swing on some bunker shots.

On the other hand, you can't become so languid with this swing that you decelerate at impact. That's why the finish position is also important. Be sure that you come through the ball and raise your hands into a high follow-through. When you've done that it means that you've accelerated through the ball and imparted the force necessary to lift it out of the bunker and to the flag.

When you play this shot properly, the ball will fly to within a couple of feet of the cup, take one bounce, and then drop like a bean bag.

63

Take a Stab at Short Shots

The next time you have one of those nightmare lies in sand, where the ball is semi-buried and you have only a metre to go to the flag, take a 'stab' at it.

This is a wonderful little shot because it floats out softly rather than scooting across the green as most shots do from this type of lie.

Traditional instruction tells you to use a square clubface when the ball is not lying cleanly, to help you dig down and unearth it. I disagree. If you have the guts to play this shot with an aggressive swing, you're better off with an open face because it will give you a softer flight.

But the real key to this shot is the stab itself. Playing from an open stance, with the ball about midway between your feet, make a wristy backswing with your hands going to shoulder height. Then on the downswing, slug the club down into the sand about 2 centimetres behind the ball and try to leave it there, just as if you were stabbing with a knife. With the open clubface, you'll penetrate the sand with the heel of the wedge, and if you stab down with sufficient force the displaced sand will raise the ball lazily upward.

OPEN

64

Seve's Softee

When you have a good lie but you need to make the ball climb quickly and stop quickly, here's a sort of trick shot to try. I learnt it from the game's finest shotmaker, Seve Ballesteros. It's played from the same address position as a basic bunker shot: open stance, open, laid-back clubface, ball positioned off the left instep. The backswing is also the same as for most bunker shots, a wristy, pick-up of the club. On the downswing, however, the secret is to loosen the grip in the last three fingers of the left hand. Don't let go – just lighten up on the grip pressure, to allow the right hand to flick the club quickly under the ball and upward, raising it sharply into a high, floating flight.

One warning: Don't try this except from a clean lie. When you loosen your grip there's a chance that the sand will grab your club and keep it there, along with the ball. For this reason also, be sure to swing through firmly and fully.

65

Slice an 8-Iron

Here's a shot that will stun your friends and opponents. It's also a great alternative to have when you're faced with one of the game's toughest assignments – the long bunker shot.

When most golfers are called upon to hit a greenside sand shot of 15 metres or more, they resort to a sort of power blast, taking a huge swing while also trying to minimize the distance they hit behind the ball. For obvious reasons, that is a risky shot. To pull it off, you need a lot of talent and a lot of guts.

As an alternative, I've developed a sort of secret weapon – the slicing 8-iron. You can't hit this shot when you have a high lip to clear, but in all other situations I think it's a better shot than the big explosion.

Basically, the idea is to make a big shallow cut across the ball, and slice it to the green, where it will spin to the right. You begin by setting up in an extremely open stance, while also allowing for the slice by aiming a bit left. As a result, your body will be aligned farther to the left than for any other shot in the game. The 8-iron also will be wide open and laid back, with the ball positioned off your left instep. Figure on opening the leading edge of the clubface about 45 degrees from square.

Grip the club at its full length, and don't be afraid to make a full swing at the ball. Just be sure that you strike the sand at least a few centimetres behind the ball. Don't worry about digging in for too much sand – your ball position and open clubface will prevent that.

If you hit this shot properly, the ball will take off well left of the target and fade slightly before it hits the green. Then watch what happens. It will take one bounce, after which the sandpaper sidespin you've applied to the ball will take effect, and the ball will scoot to the right faster than any other shot. The first time you pull this off, you'll amaze yourself. After that, you'll amaze everyone else.

66

How to Play the Hardest Shot

As far as I'm concerned, the hardest bunker shot is the severely downhill lie. Invariably the assignment is to get the ball up quickly while the slope is working hard against you.

Still, there's no reason to bail out with a chip shot to the side, if you know the proper technique. Begin by playing the ball well back in your open stance. Depending on the severity of the slope, the proper position could be as far back as your right toe. This will leave your hands well ahead of the ball and most of your weight on your left side. It will also take much of the effective loft off your wedge, so compensate for this by opening the blade wide. On this shot more than any other, you'll need to pick the club up quickly and return it steeply to the sand. You'll also have to strike the sand closer to the ball than usual.

The common error on this shot is to blade the ball into the face of the bunker or over the green. But if you make a point of hitting down hard, then you'll be able to get the wedge under the ball, and that action will lift it up and over the lip.

The Best Two Hours
You Can Spend

Would you like to know the fastest way to take several strokes off your game? Spend two hours in a bunker. Two hours is all it takes to raise yourself out of the fear-and-doubt group (about 90 per cent of all golfers) to the point where you can play from sand with confidence.

In truth, bunker play isn't that difficult. As Walter Hagen said, it's the only shot where you don't have to hit the ball. But the best way to learn is to teach yourself, by experimenting with varying ball positions, degrees of openness in your clubface and shaft, and lengths and paces of swing. Each combination of these elements moves the sand – and thus your ball – in a different way. In the course of a two-hour session you'll arrive at an understanding of this bunker-play physics, and in the process you'll discover how to play several different shots.

68

Slash Your Way Out of Jail

When you're playing from a poor lie around the green, your first concern is usually to get the ball up and out, whether it's out of a divot, a depression, sand, or heavy grass. Fortunately, all of these jails can be escaped with the same shot – and that shot is an unlikely one – a slice.

Yes, the way out of trouble is similar to the way most golfers get into trouble. When your ball is sitting down, you need to cut it out, with the same out-to-in blow that causes a banana ball.

Open up your stance so that your feet, knees, hips, and shoulders are aligned at least 20 degrees left of your target, and position the ball a bit farther back than you usually do. For me, that's just in back of my left heel. The open stance will set up the outside-to-in swing, and the ball position will encourage the downward blow.

Grass Knowledge

It's no secret that the bent grass greens common to the northern tier of the United States putt much differently than the Bermuda grass of the South. The long-bladed bent is like long hair – the ball rolls along the arcing blades of grass – whereas the short-bladed Bermuda forms a sort of crew cut, with the ball rolling along the tops of the bristles. These bristles create much more grain than do the waves of bent grass and therefore have a far greater effect on the roll of a putt. On some southern greens, a putt against the grain must be hit twice as hard as a downgrain putt.

Although less talked about, the difference is equally marked on fairways and in the rough. The ball tends to perch on the top of Bermuda fairways and sit a bit lower into bent and other types. As a result, you get clean hits and more backspin – and sidespin – on Bermuda, but slightly more distance on other types of grass, where a bit of grass gets between the clubface and ball, reducing spin.

In Bermuda rough, it's often a matter of survival – the thick, gnarly blades grab your club and slow it down, so in many cases your best bet is to cut your losses and simply chop the ball out with a short iron. In other grasses, the challenge is one of variety. You can get thick and difficult lies, as in Bermuda, but you can also get several kinds of flyer lies, which means there's most opportunity for creative shotmaking.

BERMUDA

OTHER

70

Debunking Flyers

Traditional golf instruction tells you that when your ball is sitting in light rough, you have what's called a 'flyer' lie. At impact the grass will come between your clubface and ball, producing a shot with little backspin – sort of a knuckleball. The ball will fly farther and bounce more actively than a crisp shot from the fairway.

That's true – but only with certain clubs. I've found that on short irons (PW, 9, 8) I get true flyers only part of the time. The rest of the time I get bloopers – the ball goes up quickly but then drops down quickly, and the overall distance isn't any greater than on a fairway shot with the same club.

The middle irons (7, 6, 5, 4) are the true flyer clubs. The ball consistently zings off these clubfaces and jumps into the air, arcing forward as well as upward. It comes down with very little backspin and then bounds forward. Once in an Australian tournament I hit a 250-metre 5-iron from a flyer lie, and I'm sure you've had similar experiences.

But once you get down to the long irons – anything from the 3-iron down – the flyer effect virtually disappears. The reason is that the heads of these clubs aren't deep enough to allow the ball to slide up the clubface at impact. As a result, you get either a normal distance shot – if you're lucky – or a fluff, as the ball and/or club gets caught in the grass. The fact is, you can usually hit a 5-iron from the rough as far as you can hit a 3-iron from the same lie. For the same reason, you should be careful with fairway woods from grassy lies: a 3-wood rarely works, a 4-wood has a good chance, but a 5-wood is ideal.

8 MAYBE

5 YES

2 NO

71

How's It Growing?

Just as important as the depth of your lie in the rough is the direction in which the grass is growing. When the blades of grass lean toward your target, it's usually a big advantage. More often than not, this type of lie is what might be called a superflyer. The grass at the back of the ball won't impede your club much, and the ball will jump quickly out of its nest. With such a lie, you're wise to take two clubs less than usual.

When the grass is growing against you, you have a bigger problem. Generally speaking, you'll have to take less club from this lie as well, but as a matter of survival. You'll have to hit the ball with extra force if you hope to get good distance, and in the worst of lies you'll have to cut your losses and simply wedge back to the fairway. Whenever you're playing against the grain of the rough, be sure to position the ball well back in your stance, to facilitate the necessary downward chop. Also, keep a firm grip on the club with the last three fingers of your left hand, so that the blades of grass don't twist the clubface out of alignment at impact.

72

The Lazy Lob

Nine times out of ten, when a pro golfer misses a green, he hopes to catch a bunker. We can apply spin from a bunker, play all sorts of different shots to get the ball close to the hole.

But when our shot goes wide of both the green and the bunker, we face a tall assignment. More often than not, the ball nestles into rough, where imparting backspin is next to impossible. And when the ball must be lofted back across the bunker to a tight pin placement, there is only one shot that can save you.

That shot is the lob. Ironically, it's played in almost the same way as a bunker shot, from an open stance and with an open-faced sand wedge. From there, it's a matter of sliding the clubface under the ball to produce a high shot that stops soon after it hits the green. But since you can't apply any backspin to make the ball stop, you must 'soften' this shot with the pace of your swing.

The key word is 'lazy'. The lob must be hit with the slowest tempo of any shot in the game. To develop this pace, think of making your downswing the same speed as your backswing. If your ball is in deep rough, you'll have to swing a bit more forcefully than if the lie is good, but in any case, the best way to play this shot 'aggressively', to finish close to the hole, is with a very non-aggressive swing.

73

Living with Divots

It can be frustrating to hit a perfect drive and then find that your ball has come to rest in a divot. But take heart, not all divot lies are difficult. For instance, when your ball stops at the front of a divot, you have room to get the club in behind the ball. This can often be a good lie in disguise, as it enables a very clean contact – in fact, when you can squeeze the ball between the club and the front of the turf for a split second, you can often put extra height and spin on the shot.

In the back of a divot, however, you have problems. In this situation I'll sometimes take a 9-iron or wedge and intentionally hit it thin – skull it – assuming there's no big trouble in front of the green. When you need some loft from this lie, chop down on the ball as if you were coming out of heavy rough. Just take one club more than normal so you don't have to swing too hard.

When your ball leans against the inside of the divot, the heel of your club is going to grab and probably shut the clubface down. Usually, I'll aim a little right to compensate. If it's on the outside of the divot, the toe of the club will tend to catch, opening up the face. In this situation, it's wise to aim a bit left.

74

Go Ahead, Have a Blast

Your ball has trickled into the edge of a water hazard. It's not totally submerged, but the situation looks bleak.

Don't be afraid of playing this shot – a little water never hurt anyone.

Most golf teachers will tell you not to attempt to explode a ball that is more than half submerged, but I think you can go ahead and give it a whack as long as at least some part of the ball is above the surface of the water.

Second, be careful of your club selection. You may have heard that you should play this shot with a pitching wedge because of its ability to knife down into the water. All I can say is I've tried it, and it doesn't work for me. True enough, the club cuts into the water, but then it wiggles around like a fish instead of continuing to descend to the ball. The sand wedge, on the other hand, uses its flange to disperse the water and blast a path to the ball. After all, the shot is played exactly like an explosion from a bunker – and that advice should extend to the choice of club.

But the best way to learn this shot is to practise it. You say you don't want to get your clothes messed up? Then save this shot for a rainy day. Next time you're caught in sloppy conditions – and already a mess – take a couple of balls and give the water blast a try. You may not use the shot often, but when you play it successfully, it can really give you a lift.

75

Lean Against the Slope

You hear all sorts of advice about playing from hilly lies, but what it all comes down to is this: keep your balance. Do whatever you have to to avoid falling forward, back away from, and into the ball.

Balance has always been one of the keys to my swing. People often wonder how I can take my rather narrow stance, swing as hard as I do, and not sway or topple off the ball. I think the reason is that I've been blessed with good balance. I grew up doing a lot of waterskiing and surfing. I've done loops in fighter planes and been on hundreds of fishing boats in all sorts of seas, yet I've never had motion sickness.

But when I get a hilly lie, even I have to pay extra attention to what I'm doing. The basic idea is to make sure your weight at address is leaning against the slope. On an uphill lie, put a bit more weight on your left side – flex your left knee a little more if that helps. Don't change your ball position or anything else. Just lean into the upslope a bit. This will counteract a tendency to fall backward off the ball as you take the club away.

When you're hitting the ball off a downhill slope, shade extra weight onto your right foot – flex your right knee a bit more if it helps to give you that sense of balance.

From either of these lies, do yourself a favour and take a practice swing. This dry run will probably remind you of the other important key when playing from hilly lies – keep your swing compact and controlled.

76

Three Tips for Playing in Rain

When the clouds open up and it suddenly starts raining in the middle of a round, don't think of yourself, think of your clubs. Before you put up your umbrella or dig your rainsuit out of your bag, be sure that the top of your bag is covered. When you can't get a decent hold on the club, you can't put a solid hit on the ball. An amateur golfer friend of mine actually carries a chamois cloth to rub down his grips – that's a great idea – and I'm frankly surprised I've never seen it on the Tour.

Second, when the ball and turf are wet and the grooves of your irons are filled with water, don't expect to put much backspin on the ball. You'll get a semi-flyer shot, but you won't get more distance than usual because the weight of the rain will cancel the spinless flight of the ball. In fact, on approach shots it's generally wise to take one club more than normal and make a controlled, balanced swing to guard against slippage.

My final tip is on putting. When a ball sits in the rain for more than a few seconds, its dimples fill up with water, and the result is that you will not be able to make clean club-to-ball impact. It will slip and slide both on impact and during its initial roll. So do yourself a favour and keep the ball dry for as long as possible. This means lining up your putt with a marker in place instead of the ball. Don't set the ball down until you're ready to address and stroke the putt.

77

Into a Hard Wind,
Take a Light Grip

Make a tight fist, and notice how the muscles and tendons in your forearm tighten. Unclench the fist, and your forearm loosens up again.

That's important knowledge for your golf swing. Grip the club tightly, and your whole swing will become taut and stiff. Your arms will not move freely, your shoulders will tend to tilt rather than rotate, and you'll have trouble squaring the clubface to the ball. At best, you'll rob yourself of power. At worst you'll develop a horrendous slice.

Grip the club lightly, however, and you'll be taking the first and perhaps most important step toward a rhythmic, free-flowing swing. I particularly recommend this when you're playing into a headwind, where the common tendency is to tense up for a big, hard swing. Instead, no matter how hard the wind is blowing, keep a light hold on the club. It's a nice way to fool Mother Nature.

LIGHT

78

Don't Fight Crosswinds

Some of my colleagues on the pro circuit like to play shots that counter a wind – they'll try to figure out the wind speed and direction, then try to figure out how much cut or draw to put on a shot in order to negate the breeze and produce a straight ball. In my book, that's much too complicated. When you're playing in high wind, things are tough enough – adding complexity to your shot planning will just aggravate the situation.

There's only one reliable way to play a wind – ride it. On right-to-left winds, I'll aim to the right and let the ball drift back; on winds from the left I'll aim left and ride it in that way. It'll go farther and roll a bit more, but you should enjoy and use that help from Mother Nature rather than trying to cancel it with a fancy shot.

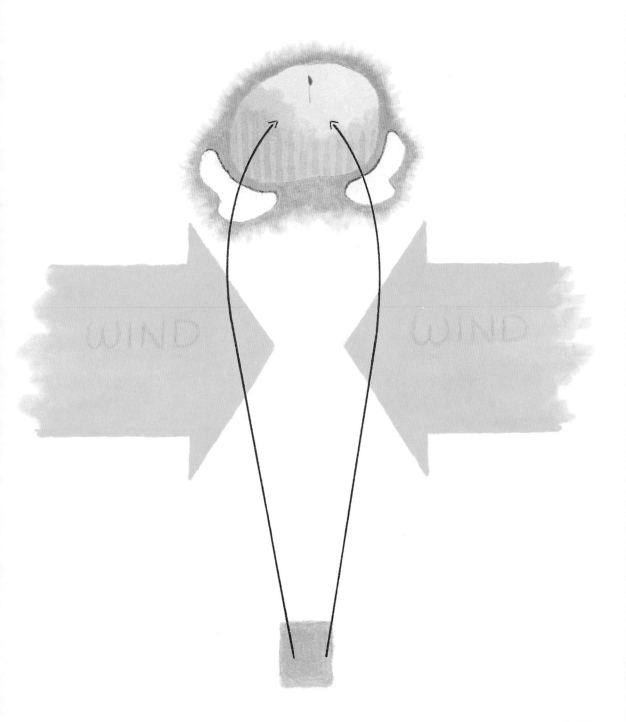

PART FIVE: MANAGING YOURSELF AND YOUR GAME

79

Know Thyself

At the end of each season, I take a pencil and paper and make a brutally honest appraisal of the state of my game. If you're serious about wanting to improve your play, you should do the same thing.

Divide your game into driving, fairway woods, long irons, middle irons, short irons, wedge play, bunker play, chipping, putting, and trouble play. Then give yourself a handicap in each area. If you're a 15-handicap overall but have a reputation as one of the best putters in your club, go ahead and give yourself a 5 or maybe even a scratch handicap in putting. But be honest on the other side too – if bunkers have you completely baffled, don't rate yourself better than a 30 in the sand.

This exercise in honesty will do two things for you. Number one, it will instil you with a feeling of confidence in the areas of your game that are relatively sound. Even if you already have that confidence, the exercise of actually writing a low number next to your strengths will reinforce the feeling. Secondly, by coldly and candidly recognizing your weaknesses you'll be taking the first step toward strengthening them. From this point, you can establish a game-improvement agenda for the next season – lessons, drills, golf school, a practice programme, etc. Whatever it may be, it should focus on these acknowledged weak points of your game.

DRIVER
FAIRWAY WOODS
LONG IRONS
MIDDLE IRONS
SHORT IRONS
WEDGE PLAY
BUNKER PLAY
CHIPPING
PUTTING
TROUBLE PLAY

H'CAP

Pace Yourself

Thirty years ago, everyone played golf by feel. Today, virtually no golfer hits a shot without first inquiring about the yardage he faces. It's a sad development in that it has slowed the pace of play among both pros and amateurs. But as long as it's become *de rigueur*, you should make the most of it.

Take an hour or so to learn the exact distances you hit each club in your bag. Your first 'step' in this process is to determine the precise length of your pace, so that when you step off distances you'll have an accurate gauge of the yardage. Take 10 steps and then get a tape measure to determine the distance. If it's 10 metres, you're lucky – one pace equals one metre – but if the distance is under or over, you should lengthen or shorten your pace to approximate a metre.

Hit a dozen or so shots with each club in your bag, beginning with the wedge. Pace off the shots for each club, and disregard the severe mishits. Average the distance of all others. If the place where you're hitting these balls has extremely hard turf, subtract the metres that the balls bounced and rolled, because the number you want for each club is your carrying distance, not your total yardage.

Once you've recorded all your distances, memorize them, or tape the yardage numbers to the shafts of the clubs. Knowing your exact numbers will take a lot of the doubt out of your approach game, and that will translate into smooth, confident swings.

CLUB	YARDS
DRIVER	270
3-WOOD	240
1-IRON	225
2-IRON	215
3-IRON	205
4-IRON	190
5-IRON	180
6-IRON	165
7-IRON	155
8-IRON	143
9-IRON	135
P-WEDGE	125
S-WEDGE	100

81

Get the Stiffest Shaft
You Can Handle

The most important consideration in purchasing golf clubs is also one of the most neglected – the shaft. I am a strong advocate of getting the stiffest shaft you can handle. A stiff shaft does not whip through and close the clubface as easily as a more flexible shaft does, so you can actually swing a bit more aggressively.

Too often, it is assumed that, when a few shots with a new club stray to the right, the shaft is too stiff. The fact is, the culprit could just as easily be too thick a grip or an incorrect lie. So be sure the other elements of your club are properly fitted. Then, if you consistently fail to square the club at impact, you'll know that you do indeed have too stiff a shaft.

The only exceptions to this rule are women and weaker senior golfers in desperate need of more yardage. With a more flexible shaft, these golfers will have an easier time releasing the club at impact, and they might even develop a draw which will add a few metres of roll and distance.

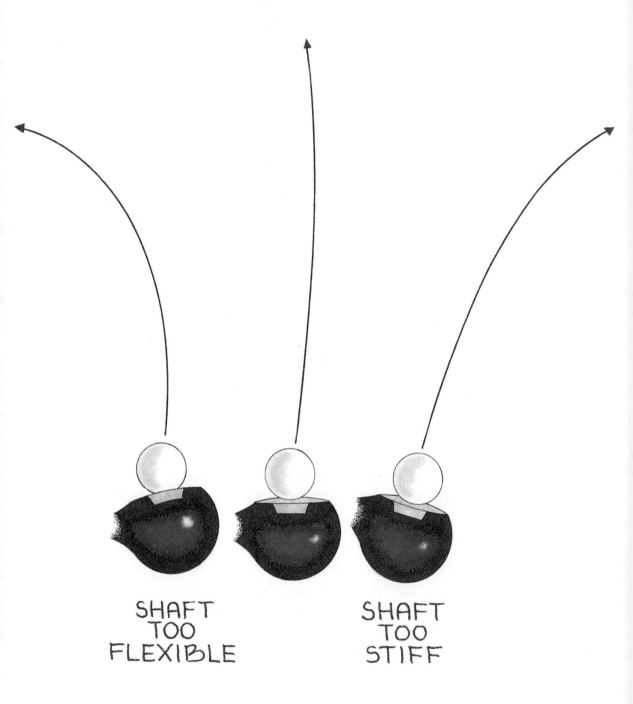

SHAFT
TOO
FLEXIBLE

SHAFT
TOO
STIFF

82

Be Bold with Your Strengths

I've often been accused of playing golf too aggressively. That's a bad rap. I admit that I play an aggressive shot now and then, but so does everyone. The fact is, my 'boldness' is simply a reflection of the confidence I have in my game, based upon experience, practice, and a knowledge of what I can do.

I've spent a good deal of time at racetracks, talked to professional race-car drivers, and driven high-performance cars for many years. As a result, I have a great deal of confidence in my ability to handle a car, and when I get behind the wheel I like to stretch my skills to a point that is equal to that confidence. Equal to but never beyond.

Likewise, on the golf course, I like to stretch my shotmaking skills, to choose the shots that I know I have played successfully time after time. That's not being overly aggressive, that's playing up to your potential.

The best strategic advice I can give you is to take note of your own golf skills and then take advantage of them. You may not be a scratch player but surely some aspects of your game are stronger than others. In these areas, be aggressive. If you have a good short game, think 'sink' on every pitch and chip you face; if driving the ball is your forte, don't feel you have to lay up on the holes where everyone else does. Display confidence in your competence, and that competence will continue to grow.

83

Pep Talks

Positive reinforcement is a term from Psychology 101, but it might as easily have been coined on the golf course. Every player likes to hear words of encouragement as he faces a tough shot, and congratulations after he pulls it off. Unfortunately, unless you play golf with your mother, you can't depend on hearing these things.

That's why I talk to myself. Not aloud, but inside my head. The tougher the shot I'm facing, the more I talk. If I'm on the last hole of a tournament, facing a long iron shot to the green and needing a birdie to win, I'll say to myself something like, 'You know this shot cold, you've knocked it stiff a thousand times, and now you're going to do it again.' Those are nice words to hear as you settle over the ball – even if they're coming from your inner self.

I also talk after I hit shots. After a particularly long, straight drive I'll often say, 'Damn, Greg, I'm pretty impressed by that one.' These inner words can be even more encouraging than the cheers of the gallery. You don't want to linger too long on your shots – good or bad – but you do want to stamp the good ones on your mind for future reference in pressure situations. Silent self-congratulation is one way to do that.

84

Go to the Movies

One key to good shotmaking is imagination. For each situation you face, you should be able to 'see' not just one shot but two or more, each with a different ratio of risk to reward.

Furthermore, for each of these alternative shots, you should be able to visualize in your mind the actual path of the ball – its direction of flight, trajectory, bounce, and roll. It's like running a mini-movie of each shot. A good player does this almost subconsciously and within seconds. Then, based upon the 'reviews' he gives these movies, he selects the most promising shot. For instance, when facing a tricky pitch to a fast green, he might reject the bump and run, after 'seeing' that the ball would roll well past the pin, and go instead with his vision of a soft-landing job shot.

Before playing my shots, I often run another movie in my mind. This last feature is a vision of a similar shot that I've played well in the past. This re-run reinforces my confidence in playing the shot at hand. It's a movie that I heartily recommend to you.

85

Why I See the Apex

For most people, the key moment in the visualization process is the end of the shot, where they imagine the ball coming down in centre of the fairway or next to the flag. I take a different view; for me, it's most important to visualize the apex of the shot I want to hit.

After all, a golf shot is not a bullet, it's more akin to an arrow. Except on the shortest of putts, I'm always playing for some sort of break or allowing for the wind, or expecting some degree of fade or draw. If my mind is beamed in on the target, I might not give sufficient consideration to these factors. Subconsciously, I might start the ball straight at the target, only to see it drift or blow or roll off to the side.

My goal is to make my ball reach the very height of its flight – or in the case of a fade or draw, the farthest point left or right in its curve. After all, this is as much as I'm able to make the ball do – ballistics and gravity do the rest.

86

Suit Your Shot to a Tee

Most beginning golfers – and even a few seasoned players – set themselves at an immediate disadvantage by perching every ball on a tee that is set at exactly the same height. The fact is, in the course of a round of golf, I may use six or more different tee heights, and so should you.

Your highest tee should be on a drive that you want to hit downwind with high trajectory, or sometimes for a shot you want to draw from right to left. Next highest is a normal tee shot with a driver. Tee it a bit lower for a slightly lower drive or one that you want to hit with a bit of left-to-right action. Thereafter, as you move through the fairway woods and irons, continue lowering the tee. On a 2-iron shot the tee should not extend more than a centimetre or so above the ground; with a higher tee, you'll tend to catch too little of the ball at impact, hitting only the southern hemisphere, and that will produce a weak shot. As the iron in your hand becomes shorter, so should the height of the peg in the ground.

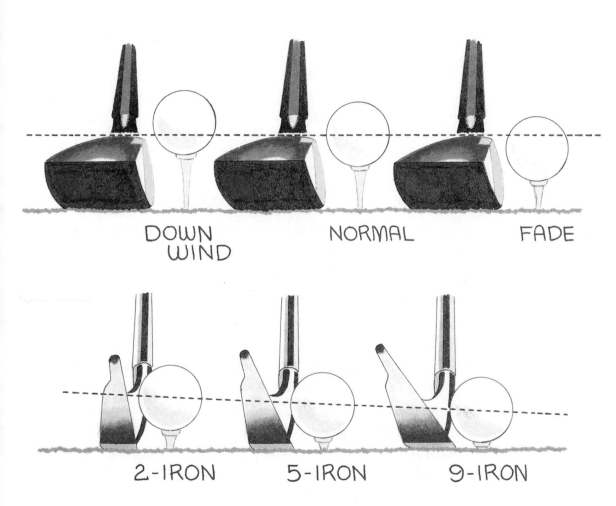

DOWN
WIND

NORMAL

FADE

2-IRON

5-IRON

9-IRON

87

The Secret Weapon

If you can't hit your driver, don't. In fact, don't try to hit any driver – go to a 2-wood. I see almost no players doing this, and it's a shame, because I think most amateurs would play better golf teeing off with a 2-wood than with a driver.

You get virtually the same distance with a 2-wood as you do with a 1-wood. The fact is, your ball will fly farther with the 2-wood than with a driver, it just won't roll as much. Overall, the difference isn't more than ten metres, particularly on today's heavily watered courses.

In addition to the added carry, you'll hit shots with greater elevation and less sidespin than with a driver. You'll also have a club with a slightly shorter shaft which makes it easier to wield and easier to hit accurately. And since you'll know you don't have the ultimate distance club in your hands, you shouldn't be tempted to swing from the heels. Knowing you have a control club should breed a controlled attitude in your swing. Finally, the 2-wood can be a valuable weapon from the fairway, especially if it's a low-profile metal wood.

Give it some thought – the 2-wood is one of the game's best-kept secrets, and it could become your secret weapon.

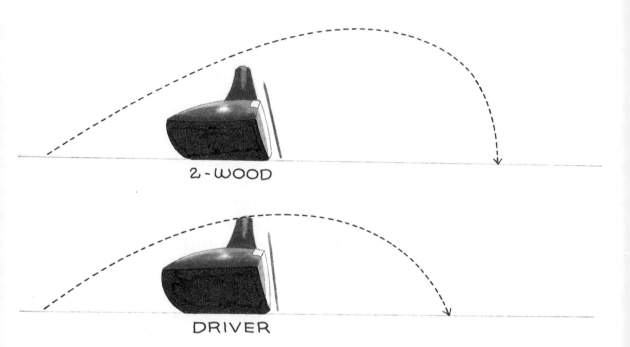

2 - WOOD

DRIVER

88

Look for 'Bad' Lies

On the first shot of every hole you have a great advantage – you can give yourself a perfect lie. But 'perfect' can vary from shot to shot. When I'm on a par three playing downwind to a hard green – usually in the British Open – I actually try to put the ball atop the forward edge of a divot and hit up on it for lots of height and backspin. Other times, I may actually give myself a flyer – play a 3-wood out of a slightly grassy lie in order to maximize the 'hang time' of the ball in the air. Of course, it's also perfectly within the rules to stand outside the teeing area, as long as your tee is between the markers.

The rules also allow you to move up to two club lengths back from the markers. I find this helpful on par threes where I'm torn between two clubs; I'll move to the back edge of the tee, where I'll feel more confident hitting the longer club.

I also look for bad greenkeeping that might give me an edge. A lie with the ball above your feet will encourage a right-to-left shot, so on holes that dogleg left, I'll try to find a slight bump in the teeing area that will put that ball just a bit higher than usual. Similarly, I'll look for a dip in the tee when I want the ball below my feet to set up a shot that will slide from left to right.

These advantages are small ones from the point of view of physics and golf ball ballistics, but mentally, just knowing that you have a bit of an edge can help you to make an extra-confident, productive swing.

89

Play the Hole Backward

As I step onto the tee, my mind goes to the green. Before I decide which club to hit or how to play my tee shot, I want to know the exact position of the flag. Once I know that, I play the hole backward in my mind.

If I know, for instance, that the pin on a par-four hole is cut on the right side of the green, behind a bunker, then the best approach to that pin will usually be from the left side of the fairway, with a shot that will not have to cross over sand. Thus, I'll want to hit a tee shot to that left side, assuming there's no dire trouble to dissuade me. This usually means I'll tee my ball at the extreme right side of the teeing area and aim slightly leftward, toward position A.

I recommend that you do this type of 'backward thinking' on any hole where you can see the location of the flagstick from the tee. It's a bit like playing pool – you use the shot at hand to set up the ideal situation for your next shot.

On a Tight Tee Shot, Get Loose

There are a couple of tee shots as the Augusta National Golf Club that consistently challenge me – number 10 and number 18. Each is a long, tight, doglegging par four, and on each hole I've hit my share of poor tee shots. On holes such as these, my goal is to stay loose and relaxed – to prevent the difficulty of the shot from transferring to my body in the form of tension and tightness.

As I wait on the tee, I close my eyes, take a deep breath, and then slowly tilt my head from side to side, lowering my right ear to my right shoulder, my left ear to my left shoulder a few times. In fact, I do this on the first tee of every tournament.

Seve Ballesteros has a tension-relieving method of another sort. It's a bit masochistic, but I'm sure it works. He folds his arms, takes a deep breath, and then presses his hands hard against the bottom of his rib cage for about fifteen seconds. When he lets go and exhales, he has a great feeling of release and relaxation. This carries over to his shot.

I see other players who let their arms drop straight down and then shake them so that their hands flap around at the wrists, and others who bend from the waist and touch their toes. Whatever sort of exercise gets you feeling loose, give it a try when the pressure is tight.

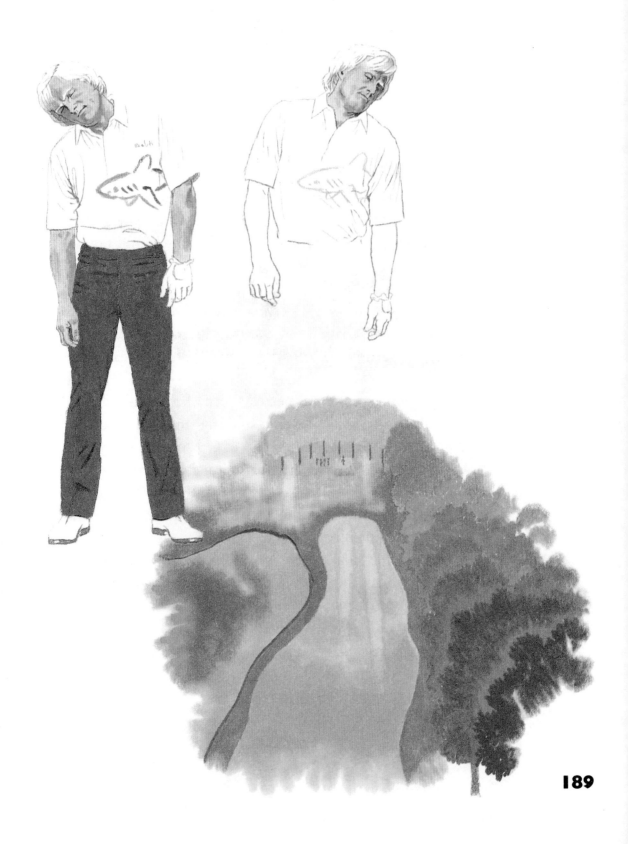

Walk Smartly

Does a pro maintain laserlike concentration during his entire round? No way. Not even Jack Nicklaus keeps the focus for four straight hours – at least not without taking a few breaks.

As I walk between shots, I let my mind wander to all sorts of non-golf things – to my wife and kids, to my next fishing trip, or whatever – but when I'm playing my best, my mind clicks back into focus well before I reach the ball.

At a point about 40 metres short of the ball I begin to analyze the situation that's facing me. I look at the tops of the trees to check the wind, I look at the pitch and roll of the green area to get an initial feel for the way the ball will roll, and I look at the people around the green to get depth perception. By the time I get to my ball, I'm fully focused on the shot.

Some of my colleagues on Tour delay this type of thinking until they arrive at the ball. I'm not saying they're wrong, but I do recommend my method to all amateurs, and for one big reason – it will speed up play!

92

3-Way Yardage

Golf may not be a game of centimetres, but modern-day golf has certainly become a game of metres. Whereas Hogan, Nelson, and Snead played essentially by feel, today's pros never hit a full shot without knowing the precise distance they have to cover.

I, of course, subscribe to this ball-to-hole measurement, but I also like to know two other distances on every approach shot I hit. First, I want to know how far I need to hit a ball to clear any fronting bunkers or hazards. Second, since I'm an aggressive player and often hit the ball with a lot of backspin, spinning my approach shots back toward the hole, I like to know the distance to the very back of the green – how far I can fly the ball and still keep it out of the trouble beyond.

For amateur players who don't have the same consistency or distance control as pros, I recommend this three-yardage approach. For each hole on your home course, it pays to know not only the pinpoint yardage but the depth of the safety zone as well.

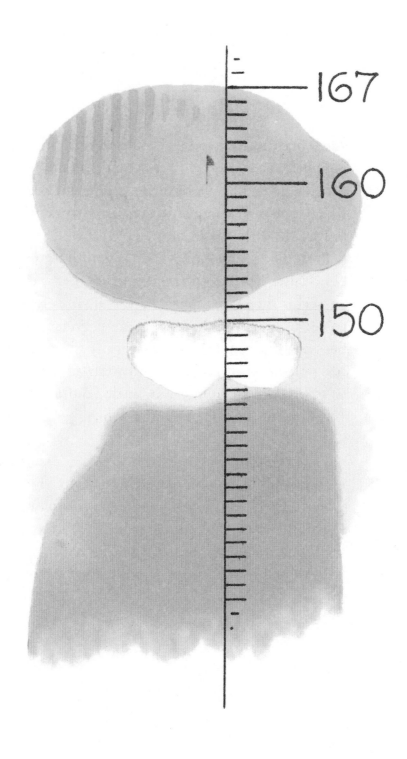

93

Yardage Is Only the Beginning

Nothing's more frustrating than to hit the right shot with the wrong club. In any round of golf you will have to make dozens of decisions regarding the proper club to hit, so it pays to know how to move beyond pure yardage and consider the more subtle factors.

Take the shorter club when (1) you're playing downhill or downwind; (2) you're playing on dry, hard fairways; (3) you're excited, angry, or for whatever reason your adrenalin is pumping; (4) the worst greenside trouble is beyond the green; (5) you're basically an aggressive player like me and you're most comfortable hitting shots full bore; (6) you're playing an intentional draw or hook; and (7) you have a lie in light rough which will likely produce a flyer.

Take the longer club when (1) you're playing into the wind or uphill; (2) you're playing to soft greens with no roll; (3) you're in a fairway bunker; (4) the worst greenside trouble is short of the green; (5) you're playing an intentional fade or slice; (6) you're a smooth-swinging player and you're most comfortable swinging within yourself.

94

Between Clubs, Go with Your Tendency

When you're facing a shot that puts you in between clubs, the usual advice is to make a smooth swing with the longer club. I think that works for some players and not others. My own general rule is to go with your first impression, whether that was the long club or the short. Your instinct is usually your best friend.

But when your instinct refuses to make a choice – or tells you that you're smack between clubs – the best choice is the one that reflects your tendencies as a golfer and person. If you're what the psychologists call a Type A personality – a hard-driving, impatient sort – you should probably take the shorter club and give it the good aggressive whack you like to use. Tom Watson is this sort of player and he always goes to the shorter club. If, on the other hand, you're a milder Type B, more like Ben Crenshaw, with a smooth swing, you'll usually do best with an unhurried pass with the longer club.

95

Gauging the Greens

On a well-balanced golf course you'll encounter greens of different sizes. Usually, the holes calling for short approach shots will have small greens. On these holes you had better select the right club and then hit the right club right. On the longer holes, however, you might encounter a green that is thirty or forty paces deep, allowing for different clubs, depending upon the pin position.

Take note of the big greens on your course, and jot down the clubs you usually play into those holes. You'll find that some will be two-club greens and others will be three-clubbers, and in these cases you should make note of the clubs for pin positions in the front, middle, and back of the green. This knowledge will help you make an accurate club selection and a confident swing.

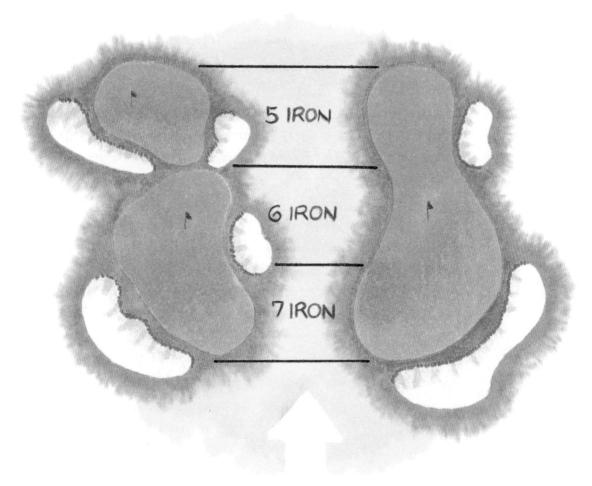

96

Don't Be a Sucker

I'm an aggressive golfer. I like to take chances. But I'm not a fool. There are certain shots I do not try. I don't go for sucker pins.

A sucker pin is a flagstick that is positioned perilously close to a bunker, a water hazard, out of bounds, a steep drop-off, or any area of extremely heavy rough. Pins cut in the spurs of greens or on the ledge of a two-tiered green are also sucker pins. If you have a fade or slice, then any pin on the left side of a green is a sucker. The opposite is true if you draw the ball – the sucker position is any pin cut near the right edge of the green.

Going for these pins is foolish because if you miss them by a little, you can put yourself into major trouble. The risk far outweighs the reward. Make note of the sucker pins on your home course, and when you come to one, give it a wide berth. Sometimes that may even mean laying up short of the green, but you shouldn't be ashamed to do it. Ben Hogan, the most accurate ball-striker of his time, was famous for such strategy.

97

Read Greens from Afar

On the Pro Tour, where we encounter a new course every week, we have to learn as much about the course as we can before the bell rings on Thursday morning. Often, the most demanding assignment is to get a feel for the speed and break of the greens. One trick I use – and recommend to you when you're playing a course with which you're not familiar – is to begin reading the green well before you reach it.

Take note of its setting. If the green appears flat but the surrounding terrain slopes in a particular direction, the green probably will fall at least a bit toward the lowlands. You should also watch the behaviour of your approach shot, and those of your playing companions. Does the ball stop quickly or take a big bounce on landing? How fast and far does it roll, and in what direction does it curve at the end of its roll? All of these things will give you hints.

Watch your companions' chip shots, too, but beware of paying too much attention to their putts. Bitter experience has taught me that each player puts a slightly different hit and roll on the ball, so I don't pay much heed to other guys' putts. But I do watch their other shots very closely.

98

My Practice Practices

When I go to the range before a round, basically I'm warming up, getting a feel for my rhythm, and determining the state of my swing. Some days I'll feel more or less loose and supple, which can mean that my shots will move a bit one way or the other. Rather than try to alter that situation in the last minutes before a round, I gear my practice to making the best of it. This is what we call dancing with the girl you brought, and it probably applies to amateur players even more than to the pros.

Also, during pre-round practice I vary my clubs. One day I'll start with the pitching wedge, then skip the 9-iron and go to the 8, skip the 7 and go to 6, and so forth, practising with only the even-numbered irons. The next day, I'll start with the sand wedge, and practise with the odd-numbered irons. I recommend this regimen to you because it eliminates the possibility that you'll become very familar and comfortable with some clubs while never getting a good feel for others.

PW 8 6 4 2   3w D

SW 9 7 5 3 1 3w D

Have a Post-round Agenda

When my round of golf is over my most serious work has just begun. Even if I've shot a 65, I'll head back to the practice tee, and always with an agenda.

More often than not, I will have played a few shots that did not make me happy. Let's say I missed two or three greens with iron shots that strayed to the left. The first item on my list will be to address that error. I'll spend at least a bucket of practice balls working on it. Once I'm satisfied that I've corrected the problem, I'll hit another bucket or so, either working on another shot or just keeping the edge on my ball-striking. Then, before calling it a day, I'll go back to the original shot, just to be sure I've found my cure.

100

Shake It Off

We all love golf, but it doesn't always love us back. No one knows better than I the strange fates that can befall you. I'll never completely banish the ghosts of Larry Mize, Bob Tway, Robert Gamez, and David Frost, or the miracle shots they pulled off to beat me. On the other hand, I can assure you that I have stored those guys and those moments very deep in the back of my mind.

What I've learned over the past several years is that there are certain things about golf you can't control. You lose more often than you win – and if you're a weekend player, you probably make more bad shots than good ones.

Shake them off. Step aside for a moment, take a deep breath, close your eyes, and do your damnedest to forget what has happened. There's no room on the golf course for anger or self-pity. The sooner you regain your composure and determination, the sooner your best shots will return.

And when things become blackest, remember the words of 1946 U.S. Open Champion Lloyd Mangrum: 'It's not your life, it's not your wife, it's only a game.'